STACEY PRICE

an inspirational story of strength, courage and hope

T0163701

FORSAKEN

WHEN ONE BECOMES TWO AGAIN

Published Brisance Books Group LLC
The publisher is not responsible for websites or their content that are not owned by the publisher.
Printed in the United States of America
First Edition January 2019

ISBN: 978-1-944194-52-9

Cover design: PCI Publishing Group

012019

CONTENTS

Chapter 1   Broken   1

Chapter 2   Who Am I?   3

Chapter 3   The Grief You Will Endure   11

Chapter 4   Get Over It   29

Chapter 5   Stop Being So Negative   37

Chapter 6   Some Days You Just Don't Know What to Do   41

Chapter 7   How I Feel Is More Important than What Is Right 45

Chapter 8   Am I Good Enough   53

Chapter 9   All Advice Is Not Good Advice   57

Chapter 10   Don't Make the Mistakes I Made   63

Chapter 11   If You Have Learned A Lesson Your Time
             Has Been Well Spent   75

Chapter 12   Add A Little Sugar to those Lemons   81

Chapter 13   Celebrate Your Victories, No Matter How Small 91

Chapter 14   I Need Something Tangible   97

Chapter 15   Life Isn't Always Unfair   101

Chapter 16   Owning Your Part and Growing Healthier   109

Chapter 17   Take Care of Yourself   115

Chapter 18   Where Pain Ends and Peace Begins,
             A New Life for You   119

to Gracey, Wesley and Sarah

You are important. You are loved.

You are my inspiration.

CHAPTER 1

BROKEN

I feel so bad sometimes, so guilty. Here I am alive and, for the most part, well. There are so many people out there with pain that I can't relate to, unbearable pain that I know nothing about. The loss of a child, a physically abusive relationship, or living out your last days in the grip of a terminal illness. Some epic tragedy that forever changed who they were and who they will be for the rest of their lives. Yes, I feel bad for complaining, hurting, crying over my loss. But my loss has also forever changed me. I know not of every loss; however, I do know of my loss. I don't dare compare it to what others have gone through. But, if you are experiencing close to what I have, then maybe we can relate.

Maybe I can explain to you that you will be alright. You will breathe, live, and possibly love again with all that is left of your heart. I know what you are thinking: *how dare you tell me I will be ok. I will not, no one can possibly understand how much I loved my spouse and family and now it is gone.*

My dear one, I understand. I don't know your personal circumstances, but I know how it feels to be crushed to the very depths of your soul. To walk the floors all night long in disbelief, wondering… *what happened?* I know what it is like to not be able to eat or sleep for months at a time. I know what it is like to not be able to stop crying, whether in private or public.

I also know of a great Healer. You can't find it in a prescription bottle, supermarket shelf, or earthly relationship. My friends, the great Healer is our God. He knows what you are going through and He is right there beside you. He is hurting alongside you and asking you to find rest and comfort in Him.

Travel by my side and let me tell you about my experience. I am not a psychologist, counselor, or Bible scholar. I am simply a woman who has had her world flipped upside down, made a lot of mistakes, and by the grace of God found myself and the true meaning of my life. I survived… and so can you.

CHAPTER 2

WHO AM I?

How long were you with your spouse? Six months, a few years, decades? Even if you were together for only a short time, you may be feeling lost, looking for your identity and constantly wondering, *Who am I?* I remember who I was throughout my life.

When I was a little kid I was Bryan and Debby's daughter. Then as I got older and entered school I was Shawn's little sister. I can think back and I see that I was labeled and defined by those who surrounded me. I don't remember having much of an identity as a younger child. I had a dysfunctional family and I didn't have many friends. I was very intimidated by people, especially kids my own age. I felt I didn't fit in. I tagged along with my big brother and his friends. I'm sure I was an embarrassment at times because I tried to be funny and fit in and I just wasn't funny and didn't really fit in because I wasn't being myself.

Which, leads me to the constant dilemma in my mind: what is myself, what does that mean? Well, when I turned 11, I finally met a friend. We moved next door to her and my brother knew her from his class as she was a couple years older than me. I only had two brothers so when we became friends it was so fun, she taught me how to fix my hair and we experimented with makeup. We also did things we shouldn't have. Like, getting into a little trouble. But I finally had a friend of my very own and we did so many fun things together. For the first time in my life I was laughing with a friend. Laughing with a friend is one of the best experiences I can think of in life.

But now, I was Wendy's friend. I was good with that because I loved having her as a friend. We still are friends to this day, although we live states—and many miles—apart. But when we do talk or see one another, it's like we never missed a beat. I can still tell her anything without the fear of judgment and I can still laugh with her about the crazy things we have done and gone through in life.

Later in my teen years we moved around a bit and I found myself in a new high school. I knew only a handful the 3,000 students who attended that school. I felt like a little fish in a big pond, to say the least. I decided I was going to try out for sports teams in hopes that I would meet some friends. I was cut from the volleyball team, for good reason—I had no idea what I was doing. Then, basketball season rolled around, and I had even less knowledge about that sport. I tried anyway, tried to fake it for sure. Well, because I was one of the taller girls and not a whole lot of girls tried out, they decided to keep me. I was excited and terrified.

Soon, I made a few friends and I fell in love with basketball. I finally had my own identity that I alone would be responsible for building. I earned the title of basketball player and I lived and breathed it for the next four years. I worked hard and for the first time in my life I felt like someone was paying attention to me and pushing me to work harder and go farther. My coach. Not long after those years of basketball were behind me, I found myself married to my first husband. I was 19, trying to finish college, working a full-time job I didn't like, and saddled with a mortgage and bills. It was a hard transition for me. I was no longer Stacey, the basketball player, now I was Mike's wife. And everyone made it clear that *I* was the lucky one. Some of his family was ruthless and made it be known that, in their eyes, I was not good enough for Mike. It made me feel like such a nobody and, before too long, I bought into the idea that I was the lesser of the two of us and my self-esteem fell. I became condemning of myself in a way that I had never been before. It is one thing growing up in a family where you felt unloved and unwanted; it was another thing to be married and constantly reminded that you aren't good enough.

The truth is that I was happy to be Mike's wife. I loved him so much, maybe too much. I overlooked red flags and bad explanations of things he had done. I wanted to believe him when he told me that he hadn't done anything he shouldn't have been doing. So, I did. I believed him even though I look back and know for sure his explanations were lies or, as he likes to call it, "skirting the truth."

Never feeling 'good enough' and weighed down by the feeling that I had no identity of my own really took its toll on me. I don't think I ever really showed the depth of those feeling to my husband, but all the years of being compared to his ex-girlfriends, being told my hair wasn't long enough, and watching him lose more and more interest in me made me feel like a hollow shell. My legs weren't as long or as shapely as his high school girlfriend's and my hair just doesn't grow long so I would cut it short to spite all the criticism. I was a terrible snow boarder, a terrible mountain biker and I was—for sure—not a cowgirl. And after so many years of being told what I wasn't, I had no idea who I was.

I never stopped loving Mike and I never stopped wanting to be his wife, but my truth became that I was just not good enough. Then, we started having babies.

I became Gracey's mom, and I was good at it. Then I became Wesley and Sarah's mom, too. Oh, how I loved being a mother. It gave me such purpose and joy. But it wasn't easy at all. I gave birth to all three children within three years and three months. I had three babies running around the house and that's not easy sometimes. There were often tears on my part from the frustrations of raising kids, but I had the perfect little family and I put them high on a pedestal. Maybe too high.

I put my family before everything, even God. Well, God has a way of revealing the truth to you whether you want to see it or not. When I discovered that my husband was cheating with my best friend I dove into the Bible. I knew that surely God would have the answers, and he did. But, when only one of the two people in a relationship is willing to follow God's word, there is no way of working things out. When Mike left me, he told me that I was too religious and, to sum it up, that I was a bad wife. I was told by my former best friend that this was not in any way her fault, but mine. I wasn't a good wife.

So, here I was 15 years after being either Mike's girlfriend or his wife… and now I had yet another new identity. And *that girl* was obviously a bad wife or this wouldn't have happened to her. I actually bought into that for a while. But, then I realized that no one is perfect and that Mike wasn't really that great of a husband. I mean if we all want to be honest here.

It's crazy the things people will tell you once you are divorced. Seems Mike had a history of having affairs dating back to before we were even married.

A very wise counselor told me, regarding not being good enough, that I am not a bad person, Mike just made a choice. I realized I was not a bad wife, he just made a choice and, in my opinion, a very bad one. I have found that when people are doing things that they know are morally wrong, they tend to justify it by blaming it on the person that they are hurting or offending. It must make it easier that way. After all, if you are having an affair, hurting your wife and tearing your family apart, it *would* be easier to justify it if you can somehow make it the other person's fault. Seems silly, but I fell for it for a while. I know better now.

So, where did that leave me? I was desperately searching for myself. I knew I was, without a doubt, my childrens' mother and I love that identity. But, there was now a piece of me that was unidentifiable. I was labeled all over my town as a divorcee and that title embarrassed me. I came from a broken home and I had decided long ago that I would never allow that to happen in my life. Well, that plan failed and I had to face it every day for the next two years.

When people I'd run into asked about my family, then I'd have to explain: I'm divorced. It's like having had a painful car crash and then having to retell the story, in detail, every week for the next few years. My life felt like one big car crash and I searched for a way out.

Everything that I had once loved to do I now had no interest in doing. No more scrap booking, sewing, or decorating the house. I threw myself into church. I found an amazing Bible study group, six remarkable and resilient women, and some of whom were in the same situation I was. People started to get to know me as Stacey, a single woman raising three kids on her own. It took a long time, but I started to feel good about the person I was becoming. I was constantly living in the word of God and I was trying to take the high road. I failed miserably at times, but having read the Bible so much I knew that if I repented and kept striving to do better and be the kind of person God wanted me to be that I was on the right track.

CHAPTER 3

THE GRIEF YOU WILL ENDURE

Let's talk about some things you will go through: Denial, anger, bargaining, depression and finally acceptance. It sounds like someone had died, instead of merely a divorce. But, divorce is a death, the death of a marriage and family. The best description of divorce came from my Divorce Care class, "Divorce is like a funeral where you will never be able to close the casket." Some people who have not been divorced see this statement as extreme and over-dramatic. I see it as fact! I lived it.

Denial came so easily to me. I just knew my husband wasn't cheating and lying. I just knew he would never leave our family and divorce me. Even after he left I was in denial, I just knew God would drop a bomb on him that would change his mind and he would call the whole thing off. After all, I was slowly becoming the person God was wanting me to be. Wouldn't that be appealing to him?

He would surely want me back when he saw how much I was changing for the better.

Wrong again! I guess when we really accept Jesus into our hearts, we truly believe God can do anything. And, believe me He can. But the fact is, God gave us free will. We can love Him or not. We can completely deny His existence or we can be on the fence about whether we believe in Him or not. That means that even if I turned into a saint by all worldly and heavenly standards my husband still had his own choice of either making our marriage work or walking away. He walked away, and God would not force him to stay.

It is almost comical looking back. I was so sure that they did not have a physical relationship. They were meeting in a "secret" spot in the woods. My husband would tell me he was going to go find some quiet time and read or think, but I knew he was going to meet her. I just hoped I was wrong. Then there was the time when he wanted to make a manly solo trip on horseback across the wilderness to the town where she lived and where we had once lived. She just happened to be camping at the halfway point that same night. At the time, I found myself turning into quite the investigator... and everything he did was so suspicious. I would find little puzzle pieces everywhere and figure it out. Most of the time I said nothing because he was so defensive and downright mean to me at the time. But the crazy thing is I still did not believe they were having a physical affair. I know what you're thinking, *Come on Stacey, you really didn't believe it?*

Looking back, I just had so much faith in and love for my husband I didn't believe he could do anything like that. One night in June we met for dinner at a local pizza place. At the time, my husband was staying at his grandpa's because he needed time for himself to think about our marriage. As we were leaving I noticed he took out his phone immediately and started talking to someone. Bingo, I knew for sure he was talking to her. When I got home I decided to log onto our cell phone account and check the phone records. When the list of calls and texts showed on the screen I was immediately sick to my stomach. This was a turning point, up until this point it had all been gut feelings and speculation. This time I had concrete proof and it hurt. It hurt like nothing else I had ever experienced. There were hundreds of call and thousands of texts. I couldn't believe how seeing this made me so physically ill, I felt like I would vomit, I started to shake and I was nervous to the point of being lightheaded. I felt as if the last 15 years of our life was a lie, like I didn't know the person that I had slept next to for the last 12 years. I had been betrayed down in my soul by someone I thought would be my partner for life.

I called my mother immediately. I asked her to come watch the kids. I knew he was going to be in the parking lot at the auto parts store changing out a part on our truck, so I was going to confront him. My mom finally arrived 10 minutes later, but it felt like hours to me. On my way to confront him—it was an eight-minute drive— the time seemed like forever. I was screaming the whole way, shouting out to the Lord, *please, please don't let this happen.* I have never heard sounds like that come out of my mouth, I was so deeply grieved. When I arrived, I walked up to his truck and he didn't even notice I was standing there. He was on the phone with her and working on his truck. I just leaned against the truck and listened to what he was saying. He was obviously talking about a recent night they had spent together and it made me sick. I heard him start talking about me, by his answers it sounded as if she asked how our pizza dinner had gone. That is when I finally summoned the courage to stand up in front of him. I just stood there when he finally noticed me, he answered her with "dinner went well, she's here right now." Then he said he had to go. That confrontation was so hard for me and I could probably tell you every little detail about it because it is branded in my mind.

The most important thing I said that night is something I will regret until the day I die. After our very long, tense conversation I told him if he came home and tried to work things out I would put all my love, faith, and trust in him. Even typing those words, I am grieved with sorrow. You see, later and through a lot of very hard lessons I learned, I realized that no one person will ever satisfy you for the rest of your days. Accepting Christ and letting God fill you is the only satisfying action of your life that will last and give you internal peace on this earth. What I said to *him*, I should have reserved for God. For one, how could I trust my husband at all if he had already proven to be untrustworthy. I could have no faith in him. I did love him, but at this point it was only because of the years and family we shared. So, I was wrong, I said something I believed I could do, but could never do. I do feel that what I said to Mike hurt God and that grieves me very much. God was rescuing me at the time and I was constantly fighting Him to save my family. I should have put all my love, trust, and faith in God and continued to be the best mom I could be. I should have let God fight the fight for our marriage. I have asked God to forgive me for putting Him second. I know I am forgiven, but it is a life lesson that when I think about it brings sadness upon my heart. I know that He loves me and the slate is wiped clean, but I am left with the memory and I will continue to use it for positive growth.

The days, weeks, and months dragged on and I continued in denial about our marriage coming to an end. He left on July 16 and never returned, divorce papers finally came in October. I had to respond. I had no money for an attorney, so I did the best I could. Often, I would read and reread the paperwork and not understand a word it said. It was if I was in a fog. The most important issue to me was the children, so I tried to get as much time with them as possible. Time seemed to pass so slowly during this point in my life. It was like a horrible waiting game. I would talk to God and remind Him that He was running out of time and He needed to do something now. Fall turned into winter and on a chilly February day I checked my mail only to find an envelope addressed to me in my husband's handwriting. I knew, from the return address, that it came from the court. I knew what it was, but I didn't want it to be. I opened it right away and saw that our divorce was final. I was a divorced woman and my husband now free to do whatever he wanted. I remember calling him right away and saying why couldn't you warn me, why wouldn't you tell me this was coming. He told me he had addressed that envelope when he submitted our paperwork months before and that he didn't know.

I took the kids inside and got them settled. The night was upon us and I needed to go out to feed the horses. I got hay for the horses on the east side of our property and grabbed a few flakes of hay for the others. At the halfway point, I remember falling to my knees. I dropped the hay and fell to the ground. I cried so hard I couldn't breathe and then began dry heaving. I just laid in the dirt hoping that I would just die right there and never have to get up again. I was visible from the road and I thought, *I hope no one sees me and tries to help*. I was at one of the loneliest points in my life and I was just positive I would never be ok again.

Motherhood has a way of making you pick yourself up and go on. I had three little ones to feed and bathe and put to bed. Such innocent kids, just four, five and seven at the time. They had no idea our family, as we knew it, was now dead. I was no longer in denial about divorce, it was done. I went in and took care of the kids. I didn't sleep that night and I cried buckets of tears. It would be days before I could tell anyone that I was divorced.

I was ANGRY! I had done everything I could do to save my marriage and with one signature from a judge it was over. My husband didn't care, he was free from me and free to start incorporating his girlfriend, my ex-best-friend, into his everyday life. Everything that I had tried so hard to keep from making me angry had built up over the past year and I'd had enough! How could God let this happen, didn't He appreciate the fact that I had done all that He was asking me to do? I know I made mistakes along the way, but I would always recognize my mistakes, ask forgiveness, and change my ways. Wasn't that enough?

I remember one night when I really let God have it. *I am angry with You*, I told Him. Then I made a list of everything from the last year that I was so mad about. I slid off my bed to my knees and then slumped on the floor. I started crying and through my tears told God that He could have changed it, with one wave of His hand he could have fixed all of this. I knew He had the power and I was so mad at Him for letting this happen. Laying on the floor crying in anguish, God knew my rantings were no more than the ravings of a child who didn't get her way. All along I knew He wanted my marriage to work as much as I did, but I also knew that He was a gentleman, someone who would never force His will on anyone. He would put up roadblocks and red flags and use whatever means He could to reason with my husband, but I knew all along He would leave the decision up to Mike. I knew God was hurting and sitting next to me crying because of my painful rant… and the fact that I was yelling at Him, the one I loved above all others. He was hurting because I was hurting. And He loved me.

What was I angry about? There is a list a mile long and for the next four years I would have to deal with every single incident, so I could finally move past it. I didn't just have to deal with the individual situation, I had to fight it, wrestle it to the ground over and over until it finally submitted to me—and not the other way around. How did I know when I finally beat each and every little memory that made me angry? I think over time I realized if I could think about a specific situation and not become stark raving mad then I knew I had made progress. And I could take that memory and either learn from it or just let it be… and not feel the need to think about it anymore. Have I beaten every terrible memory that has made me so mad? No, but I have beaten most of the big ones that hurt me to the core. Do I have days when the situation as a whole can still make me mad? Yes, but the power lies with me and not the memory. I can now choose to bring myself down and live it all over again or I can choose to put it aside and go on with my day. How did I get this power? God. He taught me through His word what to dwell on, how to forgive, and how to live in the present. I would like to say it was instantaneous—immediate—but even with God at my side my humanity makes me strive to practice and practice until I get it right. I am seeing progress all the time and I know that if I get stuck on something, I just need to look up and really work the situation out. It will always take time, but that is exactly what I have... time.

I can look back and see that I lost a lot of time to anger but, I know that if I had suppressed all the angry moments, they would only continue to pop up at certain times in my life and waste more valuable time. For whatever reason, God had me wait at those roadblocks until I worked the particular problem out. I must say that I blew through a lot of those roadblocks only to get a ticket and be sent to the end of the line to wait even longer. So, what I would like to share that is most important, is that if you are angry, work through it. If you continue to be angry then seek the help of a counselor or mentor. They can see things a lot more clearly than you, and clarity is a good thing during your life travels. Anger is a God-given emotion and He tells us that we can be angry, but we must not sin. The second part of than scripture was a hard lesson to learn and I expect I will have to continue to learn it for the rest of my life. So, remember that the next time you get angry: Try your best to not sin. That means don't call your ex or soon-to-be-ex and yell at him or her for every miserable thing they have ever done. I'm cringing as I write this because that is exactly what I had a tenancy to do. With time and patience, I have made progress in learning the second part of the scripture, not sinning, but man I can still get mighty angry.

Bargaining will also play a part in your divorce. I can remember talking to God, promising Him that I would do whatever He wanted if He would just make things the way they used to be. I also constantly bargained with myself. I just knew if I did the right things, acted the right way, stayed thin, and always had my hair and makeup just right that I could win my husband back and keep my family together.

Living everyday with the burden of bargaining is exhausting. If only I do this, then, that will happen. It is such a sad way to live, but it comes with the territory. That is why the Bible comes in handy. Learning the truth about what you mean to the Creator of the universe can be a big self-esteem booster. When you are at your lowest and all your bargaining does not pan out you should remember what you mean to God. He says in **Psalm 139:14** that *I am fearfully and wonderfully made;* (NIV Bible). Also, in **Jeremiah 29:11**, He tells me, *For I know the plans I have for you, declares the LORD, plans for welfare and not for evil, to give you a future and a hope.* A beautiful scripture from **John 3:16** tells us *For God so loved the world, that he* *gave his only Son, that whoever believes in him should not perish but have eternal life.*

I believe John 3:16 is one of the most memorized verses in the Bible, chances are even if you do not study the Bible you have heard this verse. A lot of people hear this verse and think that's nice or, possibly, they don't believe it. What would it take for a parent to offer his or her son as a sacrifice? Let me tell you my experience with this verse.

I was just like everyone else. I thought it was a touching verse and didn't give it much thought after that. One night when my oldest son was about four years old I was thinking about him. I thought how much I loved this little boy and loved to see him grow and develop his personality. I thought about what he might be like as a teenager, then a man. Would he go to college, get married, have children? I was overwhelmed with love for this boy that I had been blessed with.

Then my thoughts turned to God as I was praising Him for blessing me with this little child that had brought me such joy. A thought popped into my head, and I started talking to God. I told Him how much I loved Wesley and then I began to cry. I asked Him, *How could you send Jesus to his death for someone like me?* I love my son so much and the thought of him suffering in any way brings me to tears. *How could you do that to your child, Lord?* I sat there with tears pouring down my face and an answer finally came. God said, *I did it because I love you as much as you love Wesley.*

This may not sound profound to you, but at that very moment I finally understood how much God truly loved me. He loved me more than the pain of sending His own son to the cross. That was a huge turning point in my faith. I knew that God existed and was active in all our lives and loved us, but until that point I didn't realize the extent to which he loved me.

This idea would linger in my head throughout my divorce. I knew God loved me and I could go to that thought when all my bargaining failed and I was left feeling discarded and unloved. The God of our beautiful universe loves you, just as much as He loves me. You are worthy of His love and you don't need to bargain to stay in an unhealthy relationship. You don't have to bargain to get someone to love and care for you, because God already loves and cares for you. Your relationship with your spouse or ex-spouse may work out eventually, but you do not need to grovel and beg. Hold on to what you know—that you are fearfully and wonderfully made and that He has a plan to prosper and not harm you. You are worthy of being loved.

Along with divorce comes depression. It is different for everyone. Some people may seem like they have it all together, only to fall apart when no one can see them. They say, "I'm fine," in the hope of appeasing others, not drawing attention to themselves, or because they are embarrassed.

What follows is long periods of feeling like you want to crawl out of your skin. I remember realizing, and *knowing*, that in no way, shape, or form was I the person I used to be. I was so sad that I could not sleep in my own bed for over a year. Most nights I just couldn't sleep at all, so I would lay on the floor staring at the ceiling or walk, in circles, around the house.

I couldn't bring myself to eat anything. At my lowest weight, I had lost over 40 pounds. I remember a fall day when I realized I hadn't eaten much of anything in about a week. It really scared me and I ran to the refrigerator and tried to force down a yogurt so I would have some nourishment in my body. I had my parents very worried. One day my dad came over and burst into tears when he asked how much I weighed. It made me feel terrible. Not only was I a wreck, but I was causing my family to worry about me.

Weight *gain* also is a typical side effect of depression. Although I have struggled with my weight since I was in my mid-twenties, I had no desire to eat. My dear friend who went through a similar situation said she ate and ate because she just knew that she was unlovable and if she gained enough weight she would never have to worry about someone loving her again. Sad isn't it, how a divorce will wage war on your body and mind?

My mood was also out of control. I pushed away the people who cared about me most. I never went into much detail with my family about what was really going on during my divorce. I wanted them to somehow still accept my husband, should he ever come back. I didn't divulge all the dirty details and often got angry at them for no reason. I just couldn't stand to be around anyone, so I would isolate myself in my sad little world.

Then, on a January morning it hit me the hardest. I had one child in school and two still at home. After I got my daughter to school I made sure my other two kids had what they needed and I laid on the floor next to the wood stove. I was so cold and tired. My body hurt all over, like I had been hit by a truck. I had tears flowing from my eyes the whole day. When my daughter got home from school, I did what I needed to get by. This went on for three solid weeks.

In my life, I don't remember ever having my body ache down to my bones and being so cold I was shivering. My lack of motivation was unbearable, I literally could not bring myself to do anything other than the necessities. I told everyone I was fine, but I wasn't. During that time there was no bargaining, no anger, no actions on my part. Just complete emptiness.

Somehow, I slowly came out of it. I never want to feel that way again. This was full-blown depression and I should have talked to a doctor. If you are feeling this way, please know that you are not alone. You are not a freak, or weak… and you don't deserve to feel this way. There is help out there and I ask you to please seek it. If you are going to get through a divorce, recover, and be healthy again then you must ask for help. There is no shame in it, it is a stage of your grief and it will pass.

A day will come when the anger fades, the depression is gone, and the sun starts shining in your life again. It has been several years for me since the start of the end of my marriage. I made it through the divorce and, after two and a half years, I even remarried. However, I am truthfully able to say that only now am I starting to feel like myself again. That old familiar *me* is back— the hobbies I used to enjoy have now piqued my interest again, I don't think about my ex-husband (or my ex-friend) anymore. I don't wish I could tell them all what I wanted to tell them, how they hurt me and how much trust and love I once had for them. I have energy to do things. I find myself looking forward instead of backward. I have hopes and dreams again. And I know the truth: That I deserve to have this peace in my life and I obtained it by holding steady to God's promises.

I have finally made it to complete acceptance. I accept what happened and I choose to make myself into a better person according to God's standards. I will never again take a relationship for granted and I will not enter relationships that are unhealthy. I have regrets and I learn from them. I don't dwell on the past, but instead I use it to help guide my future. If a similar situation arises that reminds me of the past I try to make a better decision on how to handle things.

GET OVER IT

These kinds of statements can be some of the harshest and most condemning words when you are healing from separation or divorce. *Get over it?* Let's face it, there isn't a lot of positive to dwell on during this time and it is nearly impossible to see the light at the end of the tunnel. Pain and negativity seem to trump anything positive in every part of your life.

If you have friends who you constantly confide in who have never gone through a similar situation, they will grow tired of hearing your complaints and hurts.

Get over it! It is possible, you have heard this from your spouse... get over it. This is such a cruel statement and I don't think people think through what this statement really means. I believe it is something people say when they are frustrated with your pain and have no other advice to give you or way to help.

They are just popping off at the mouth in frustration with an overused, insensitive statement that they will forget they even said in the next hour. What you heard was a much more hurtful statement that will probably haunt you and make you second guess how you are feeling and leave you wondering why you *can't* just get over it.

I remember my three children coming home from their weekend visit with their father. We had only been separated about five months and since the first weekend visit with the kids my soon- to-be-ex-husband had been spending time with the kids and bringing along his mistress as well. When my five-year-old son started telling me about the weekend I could tell he was upset. He said, "Mommy, me and Sarah told Daddy that you cry all the time for him. He said you need to get over it." I could tell at that very moment that his father's statement had hurt him as much as it had hurt me. My son was angry. It was obvious to me that he was grieving over how badly I hurt and the fact that I could not stop crying. I could not get over it.

I would like to ask people what they think is the adequate time frame for getting over it? Does it depend on how long you were married, the details of the break up, or your emotional sensitivity? I was married for 12 years, together with my ex for 15 years, and had 3 children together. So, can someone please tell me when I am officially supposed to *get over it*?

The fact is, I have had such loving, supportive friends—as well as some not-so-loving friends—utter this disturbing statement to me. In their defense, I am sure I was absolutely no fun to be around for a few years after my separation and subsequent divorce. And I know I was in so much pain that it hurt them to see me, talk to me, or try to help me. And in frustration they offered what they might have believed was tough love: They told me to get over it.

If you are in this same situation, please don't think you need to get over it. But, remember there is a healthy, pain recovery process that you can go through that will allow you to move past this divorce or there is a deep and dark place that you can live in. The choice is yours. I have lived in both places. I have chosen to pick myself off the floor and live for the day and I have also chosen to lay on the floor all day and resonate in misery. I think both places are part of the process, regardless of how strong and healthy a person you are.

It has been years since my ex-husband walked out the door and I still haven't gotten over it. Let me tell you what I *have* gotten over. I have gotten over loving him and wanting him back. It was a long process and with prayer and time all the in-love feelings have left and the desire to reconcile our marriage has disappeared.

A very difficult thing to get over is the rejection. Rejection is so hard for any human being, man or woman, to take. It was like I put my every heart in the hands of one man and he didn't think twice about dropping it to the floor. Making a vow with someone before God, family, and friends is a very serious endeavor. Breaking it seemed to be the easiest thing he ever did. There were no tears on his part, no apologies, no remorse. I remember sitting on the kid's trampoline outside one June afternoon, after I had confronted him about all his phone calls to his mistress. He turned on me and said he had nothing but distain for me and that I disgusted him. Talk about rejection—and by the only person who had promised to accept me as I am. That one is hard to get over.

The fact is, I am finally completely over the rejection. It took time and it took me being honest with myself. Did I really want someone who would do the things this man did and speak to me the way he did for a husband? No, I don't. Would I have tried my hardest to forgive him and work it out with him? Absolutely. However, if we had stayed together I would still be working on getting over the rejection, just under different circumstances.

Let's talk about getting over who your spouse left you for. That would be my best friend at the time. My husband was having an affair with my best friend, his best friend's wife. It is sad to think of it and it makes me feel like I should be featured on a dysfunctional-relationships reality show. This was a tough one to get over. When I confronted her over the phone during the affair she told me that it was all my fault because I was a bad wife. This is also what my husband was telling me. It took me a few years to realize that it wasn't me who was the bad person, or a bad wife. Yes, I absolutely was not perfect and made some awful mistakes. But I was not a bad person because of it, and it certainly did not justify my husband and best friend having an affair and ruining two marriages and forever altering the lives of five children. The fact is, they wanted to be together and they made a choice. They knew it was wrong, so they needed someone to pin the blame on in order to make themselves feel better about their horrible decision. This is such a simple truth, and those two have so many underlying demons they need to face. The truth for me, if I remember to keep it simple, allowed me to get over that my husband left me for another woman.

All in all, getting over it is a huge statement with many intricate nuances. You will have to take it piece by piece, find what triggers your sadness and anger, and focus on getting better one detail at a time. Do I think I will ever totally get over it? I really don't know. I have a huge heart for my children and I have seen what they have had to go through. And even though the divorce is over and I am remarried and we have gone on to live the most normal life we can, my children have hurts that pop up when I least expect it. My children being hurt… that's one thing I don't believe I will get over. It's one thing to break the heart of an adult, it's another to break the hearts of three innocent children. That I promise you, I will never get over.

Something I often face is the lingering question of *If I am over it, why does it still hurt?* For me the answer is simple: I will forever grieve the loss of my family. Even though the five of us are all still alive, my husband killed our family when he left. I think back to the way things were and it breaks my heart every time to know that my children have lost their family, that our family is gone forever. That one hurts, and I don't foresee getting over it. However, I can control it. I am able to put it in a special place on my proverbial shelf of life. Sometimes, in a weak moment, I take it down and wonder what our family would be like today if things had not gone so awry. I cry, too, sometimes and I get really, angry. And sometimes I smile and am thankful for the time our family did have. I laugh at the silly things that had happened and I pray that I can pass those good memories on to the kids in ways that they will embrace and cherish. Then I take my old-family box and put it back on the shelf. I feel as though I am stronger every time I take it down and can put it back. I feel lighter, less hurt, and less bitter after this process.

Sometimes I think people have it all wrong. It seems they want you to close the door and never look back, never open that door again. But I say, leave the door open to the positive things and learn from the negative. If you deny the past you set yourself up to repeat it in the future.

CHAPTER 5

STOP BEING SO NEGATIVE

Bet you have heard this one too! Your response may be, *Try walking in my shoes and not being negative.* When your whole life is crumbling before you, it is hard to be anything *but* negative. I think we tend to dwell on what our spouse did wrong or what we did wrong—or both. So, we end up constantly belittling ourselves or our spouse. Who do we do this in front of? Our mirror, our friends, family, or an unsuspecting innocent bystander. Then, we walk away feeling worse than we did before and possibly scaring the neighbor away for good! I knew, over the course of my ordeal, that I have said too much to too many people about my whole situation and I can't help but think that my emotions took a toll on my relationships with everyone in my life. I've found that our friends often walk away feeling worse, wishing they could help but feeling helpless. That is a hard thing for a friend to take and eventually, if we continue with the negativity, our friends will get tired of it and relationships begin to deteriorate as bad feelings start to grow.

How do I not be negative? That's what you are saying, I know. I was there too. I think the negativity is a natural thing that we experience, but we can let it get the best of us if we dwell on it. And, in a divorce, our dirty laundry tends to be aired in different stages, over years and years, in some cases. So, our negative trains of thought keeps going. I have not yet mastered the art of combating this problem, but I have recognized that it is a problem and that was a breakthrough for me. After one of my best friends sent me a 'stop being so negative' text I was heartbroken and offended. I was thinking: *How could I not associate everything about my ex with negativity?*

My ex continues to do things that affect the two-family dynamic negatively, so I felt justified in my negativity. But the fact is, I was negative with my best friend one too many times. I must take into consideration that she has a great marriage, has never been through an affair, separation, or divorce. She has always been there for me, but I realized I had burdened her with far more than she could handle simply because she has never been down any of those roads. So, I have learned that there are certain people I can only say certain things to. This may seem like these are shallow relationships, but I feel it is valuing and respecting the other person's boundaries. If I am to nurture and grow a healthy relationship, then I cannot feed this relationship small bits of poison and expect it to thrive. My good friend has also taught me to strive to not be negative—which is a hard lesson, but a good one. I can absolutely find the positive in most situations if I want, and she helps me want to do that more often.

On the other hand, I have another wonderful friend who had gone through nearly the same exact situation as I have, just 10 years earlier. I have the freedom to confide in this friend so much more in regard to my negative feelings. It does not mean that misery loves company, it means that this friend has a solid foundation for listening to me and offering advice or just an understanding ear. Most of the time I walk away feeling better and able to see the good in the situation. Does this friend feel overwhelmed? No, I see in her a bittersweet satisfaction that her past divorce situation was not entirely in vane because she can now help others.

Life can be full of negativity and we can choose to embrace or deny it. I say take a good, long and hard look at your negativity and deal with the parts that are going to make you into a better person and realize that some of the negativity needs to be let go of for your own healing. I can't tell you how to let go of it, I am still learning myself.

I can tell you that I wasted a lot of years holding onto it. Through prayer and counseling I have moved into a better place and have learned that every gripe and complaint does not need to be vocalized. There are important negative situations that need to be dealt with, and you must learn who to go to in those situations. The right friend, a pastor, or a counselor/mentor. It isn't easy, but when you are finally able to stop thinking about the things that make you feel angry or sad or rejected then you can take a step toward living the positive side of your life.

CHAPTER 6

SOME DAYS YOU JUST DON'T KNOW WHAT TO DO

Not all your days are full of excitement. Not all of them are something to write home about. Some days are just plain blah. There really isn't a lot going on, but there is a feeling that you can't quite put your finger on. *Am I sad? Am I depressed? What is it?* I don't know what it is, precisely, but it sure makes us want to check out for the day and do nothing.

For the most part, things are ok. It's just an ordinary day and I know I should feel happy and blessed. I should think about the fact that I have three healthy kids, a second husband who loves me, and a job where I am valued and needed. But all I can focus on is the emptiness in my heart.

After the initial pain was over and there was no more fighting or crying every day, I just didn't know what to do with myself. I entered real life again, I didn't focus on the pain much anymore… but there was something eluding me. I just seem to be a different person. And I don't want to go back to who I was. I was continuing on the road to becoming a better person, but I had no motivation to do anything and there were few things that could hold my interest.

Those days can be progress squashers, after you have worked so hard to claim a life for yourself and you can't seem to find interest in anything. Your old hobbies no longer interest you and you don't have the interest in learning anything new. You feel like you are stuck in a rut with no substantial progress in your life.

Well, let's think about it for a second… I know that I personally spent two straight years on edge day and night. I was always waiting. Is my husband going to stop cheating? Is my husband going to come home? Am I going to get divorce papers in the mail today… and when will I have to go to court? Will this be my first year of holidays without my kids; how will I feel? You see what I mean? I was so busy with all these new and scary expectations and experiences that I was rarely ever able to just relax and enjoy myself—or even *think* about something that would be fun or a new hobby I might want to pursue. I was so busy being on guard that I stopped living and enjoying life.

Of course, there were those special moments when I could forget about all the drama going on around me and enjoy myself, but when those moments passed, the guarded feeling and anxiety would return. So, it made sense to me that when everything died down and normal life was upon me again, the days would seem boring and nonproductive. I had time to do things and enjoy life, but I had forgotten how to do that.

I had definitely changed as a person and the activities and hobbies I once participated in and the things I used to enjoy doing no longer interested me. That left me feeling like I was waiting for something to happen, not necessarily in an anxious way, but nonetheless, a sense of *waiting*.

This waiting has finally turned around for me. It took five years, but I finally started to enjoy life again and appreciate time by myself. I like to walk at the park and listen to music. I really love planting grass and caring for my lawn, something I did before my divorce that I thought would never bring me joy again. But it has. I like doing things with my family, going to the pool in the summer, cooking a good breakfast for my family in the mornings. They are not big things, but they bring me joy and purpose.

Sometimes I feel like these things aren't enough, like I should be out there doing something amazing for God and society. But I have become reconciled with the fact that God doesn't expect me to save the world. He only expects what I can give for the day. Sometimes what I can give for the day is a good meal for my family and a few minutes to enjoy watching the sprinkler water the lawn. It isn't much, but as time goes on I know He will use me in bigger ways. He has made it clear to me through prayer and scripture that my family is my ministry and that is very important to me. If I can leave this world knowing I raised three healthy, well-adjusted, God-loving people that broke the chains of a broken-family cycle, then that is the biggest accomplishment that I could ever hope for.

HOW I FEEL IS MORE IMPORTANT THAN WHAT IS RIGHT

How do you feel about the title of this chapter? I'll tell you how I feel: angry. I am so frustrated with people making huge life changing decisions based on how they feel at the moment. Because you know what, give it an hour and your feelings will change.

I'm not down on feelings. In fact, quite the opposite. I am the queen of feelings. I don't know why, but God gave me the ability to feel way more than the average person. When I was a child all I ever heard was *You're too sensitive, You're too emotional… You get upset too easily*. So, all my life I have felt like I have always been different, a freak of sorts, and like there was something wrong with me. As I have grown into an adult—and especially in the last few years—I have realized that there is nothing wrong with me. Because I *am* so emotional and sensitive, I have the ability to feel things a lot of other people don't. That said, I also have the ability to show a lot of compassion for others and sensitivity to their situation. I was once told I would make a good Psych nurse because I take the time to really listen.

I once had a man tell me that it was so nice to talk to me because I was listening and not just waiting to jump in and share my opinion. My counselor once told me a very personal story and then said, "I don't know why I told you that, I have never told anyone but my family that story." I'm not saying I'm some sort of listening whisperer. I have just realized, through people who God has put into my life, that these qualities that have been too much for people to handle over the years have had a purpose and that are not less than any other gifts God has given to people.

So, I appreciate feeling good. It's nice to not be miserable or to work so hard at relationships and jobs and all the other life experiences we have. But, I believe the things in my life that I have had to work the hardest at are the things I value most. These are the things that have made me better and stronger, and grow in the Lord.

Growing up, I don't recall ever having a passion for anything. I didn't have a lot of friends or direction. I hung out, mostly, with my brothers. When I went into high school I was terrified. I was only in the city's junior high school district before I headed to high school, so I didn't know that many people. There were almost 3,000 kids in that high school and I felt like I was floating around, lost. I decided to try out for volleyball and, having never played before, was cut the first week. I then, later that year, decided to try out for the basketball team. Again, I had never played basketball and it showed, even though I tried to pretend I did. By the grace of God, and because not a lot of girls tried out, I made the team. After my nerves calmed down and well into the season, I fell in love with the sport. It truly was my first love. I had to work so hard. I attended clinics in the off season, played spring and fall leagues, and stayed out almost every night shooting hoops at the school across from my house.

I loved the fact that the coach took an interest in me and showed me that I had to be disciplined and always work hard. I never saw much playing time in my high school years, but I grew so much in my dedication to the sport and my dedication to keeping myself in shape. I spent hours and hours with a ball in my hands—and I loved it. Did it always feel good? No.

We had to run along the canal by our school in the off season. It was brutal. Although only a few miles, it was in the heat of Mesa, Arizona and we were often running in 100-degree-plus temperatures. I hated it, and every step was so hard. Sure, I got to the point where I was in good enough shape to run it more quickly and be done with it. We had tough practices sometimes too. Sessions when I couldn't help but look at the clock and think, *only five minutes have passed?* It had seemed like an eternity.

I also remember being yelled at in practice. Not just yelled at but, on two specific occasions, totally humiliated. During my senior year, Coach saw me almost run into the starting point guard. She told me, "If you hurt her I will kill you!" She didn't take me aside and tell me this privately and politely; she screamed it out in front of the whole team. I knew instantly that I really didn't have a place of importance on that team, but I loved the sport so I hung in there even when it didn't feel good. I probably didn't have more than an hour of playing time that whole season, but the practice, pain, and humiliation was well worth every second I spent on that court.

I played basketball in college for a semester at a small junior college in Northeast Arizona. I tried out and made the team. Before too long I found myself in the same place I was in High School, the bench. Our first game was in Las Vegas and I remember it so clearly. We were an average team and were playing a team that was a pretty equal match to our ability. I remember sitting on the bench watching these girls and thinking, I am so much better than they are. I decided then and there that I would not be second string any longer. If I got the chance to go in I was going all out and proving that I deserved to be in that game. I did finally get a chance to play that game and I left all my inhibitions on the court. I was always terrified that I would mess up and I didn't have the confidence to show what kind of player I really was. But that day I felt I had nothing to lose, so I went all out. That day I discovered I was a tenacious defense player. I loved it, I made the girls I was defending so frustrated because they could not get a pass by me or get off a clear shot. I had finally found where I belonged in the game I so desperately loved.

A week or so later, at practice, I took a shot during a scrimmage. It was a shot from inside the three-point line. I was a good shooter, but I didn't make it. My coach stopped practice, grabbed the ball, and in front of everyone said I was never to shoot the basketball again unless I was inside the key. That meant no further than a few feet away from the basket. I remember some of the girls snickering and I was humiliated. Again. I scanned all the exits and wanted to run away. It was hard to breath and even harder not to cry. I felt awful. But, I still loved the game.

Later in the season our team was a mess. Most of the girls drank and did drugs. I was anti drinking and drugs, so we didn't mesh well. There were dramatic fights, way more dramatic than anything I had ever been a part of on a team. And my love of the game was soon outweighed by the stress of the turmoil. At Christmas break I left and did not return. I quit because I was unhappy with the people on the team, not the game that I loved so dearly.

I cried for the next two years, in private of course. I'm crying right now. I missed out on what could have been the start of a career that could have taken me to great places. And, by great places I mean anywhere that I could be involved with basketball. I gave it up—all because of some temporary bad feelings. I missed out on so much and I am embarrassed for the day when I will share my story with my kids and they learn that I was a quitter.

But I will also share what I see as the positive that came out of that choice. I am able to share with people how I broke my own heart by making a decision based on temporary feelings. It takes time to get things just the way they should be, time and effort. The result can be magnificent if you can fight through all the garbage. You don't have to quit, you can take time to adjust, you can ride out your commitment and join another team the next year, you can seek guidance when your feelings get to be too much to handle. It didn't need to be, I learned, so very black and white. There were choices.

The same is true for everyday life. We, as adults, make so many promises and commitments that it's amazing we have time to fulfill any of them. But, there are some that are huge and important, promises that must be fulfilled and fought for. Marriage is one of them and kids are another.

My marriage ended because of one simple statement: I just wasn't happy. Oh, how I loathed the word *happy* for the next three years. I'm thinking *Really, you're not happy so you choose to do all the wrong things in search of your happiness?* Well, that ship sailed and the realities of divorce set in, all because of feelings. I learned that I also had to tame my feelings. I wanted to lash out constantly, to hurt all the people who were involved as much as they were hurting me. But, by becoming aware of how feelings can cause a person to do and say things they don't really need to say or do, I have learned that every thought does not need to be expressed and action is not always required. I'm going to repeat this, as much for my own benefit as yours: I have learned that every thought does not need to be expressed and action is not always required. Sometimes letting a sleeping dog lie is the best thing a person can do.

The next time the urge to lash out or do something you wouldn't normally do hits you like a freight train, start practicing the art of being still. Remind yourself that it's ok to have those feelings—ok to feel angry and hurt. But, like God tells us, be angry but do not sin. God will get you through if you rely on Him and ask Him for help. I have found that if I'm patient and think the whole situation through—not stew in anger, but really analyze it—then I usually don't take any action or the action I take is appropriate. I still mess up from time to time and I know I will never be perfect at this, but I will remember how it felt when my husband was leaving and took all his anger out on me. I really do not want to hurt someone in the ways that I was hurt. And one lesson I learned at a church service one day was not to say something unless it is kind, true, and edifying. This stops me from saying a lot just because of my fleeting feelings.

CHAPTER 8

AM I GOOD ENOUGH?

If you are divorced or going through a divorce, the chances are high that you have asked yourself this question. I am sure it is different for each person, and if you have been or are in the process of a divorce it is most likely a question that plagues you. Even if you initiated the divorce I believe that you have still asked yourself that same question. I have only, ever, heard one person say that they divorced their spouse because he wasn't good enough for her. I really think that is a cover and an easier path than to dig through the dirt and bring it all to the surface. My friend, I have asked myself this question as many times as one human being can. Am I good enough?

Let me tell you that in the beginning of my separation, through the divorce process, and during part of the recovery I believed I was not good enough. I really thought that if my husband didn't want me then no one would want me. This was confirmed through shallow dating relationships I had after my divorce was final. It seemed that most everyone liked me, but no one felt I was worth investing in and always had some other woman on the backburner. That hurts and if you determine how you value yourself by how others treat you, then you will likely find that you're the one messed up by all of this.

How else do you value yourself then, you ask? Well, we should look to what God says about us. There are so many scriptures that give us affirmation that the creator of heaven and earth designed you and me perfectly. Every hair on our heads, down to every cell in our bodies. He gave us a soul that makes each of us unique and special. I bet I know what you're thinking... *Gosh, you sound just like my mom and dad.* I think this is a great correlation, because if you can understand how much your mom and dad love you or how much you love your children then you have been given a glimpse into how much our Heavenly Father loves us. As much as I love my children—and I *do* love them... I would die for them—I also live for them, I wake up every morning with the hopes of bonding with them, showing them how much I care for and love them, and I try my hardest to teach them to love one another and to be kind and compassionate. Now, try and wrap your head around this: God loves us even more. More than I could ever describe or show you.

God showed us how much he loved us by sending his only begotten son to die for our sins so that one day we can go to Heaven to be with Him. You see, God is holy and sinless, and we aren't. So, therein lies the problem. How can we be in the presence of the Lord if we are all sinners? The good Lord fixed that once and for all by having His Son, Jesus Christ, take on all the sin of the world, past and present, and die on the cross so that we could go to Heaven to be with God one day. Jesus Christ is our advocate and God loved us so much that He let Jesus die a horrific death. If you are a believer already then you probably understand how much God loves you. If you are not a believer or are on the fence about whether to believe or not, then this story may frustrate you.

How could a holy and sinless God send His son to die such a horrible death? That doesn't sound like a loving God at all. The answer is, one day it will be explained to you in a way that makes sense to you. This is not a good answer, I know, and even as a believer, it was hard for me to swallow sometimes. You see I have a son and I would do anything to protect him and I certainly would not allow him to pay someone else's debt, especially with his life. One night I was lying awake praising God for my children. Sometimes it would bring me to tears when I thanked God for my kids because they bring me such purpose and great joy. I was talking to God while thinking of my son and I told God how grateful I was for my son and that I didn't understand how He could send His son, Jesus, to be tortured and die on the cross. I was crying at the thought of it and so grateful at the same time, grateful that Jesus did die for me. I kept saying to God that I couldn't do that to my son, I just couldn't. Even if it meant that the whole world would perish someday. God finally spoke to me, and in my mind I could hear Him say, *Stacey, you know how much you love Wesley?* I said, *Yes, God.* And He said, *I love you more than that.* All at once I understood why God allowed Jesus to die so that I could reconcile with God and be allowed in His Kingdom when I die.

I finally realized how much God loved me. I am his child, too. I am not as amazing as Jesus Christ, I acknowledge unequivocally, but I *am* God's daughter and He wants me with Him, not just when I die and go to Heaven. He wants me now. He wants me to remember how special I am, how much I am loved, and how perfectly he created me. I am not perfect, not even close, but God tells me through His word that I am "fearfully and wonderfully made."

CHAPTER 9

ALL ADVICE IS NOT GOOD ADVICE

When I was in the throes of the battle to save my marriage, I had all kinds of advice thrown my way. At the time, I was in such a fragile emotional state that I listened to everything that people had to tell me. And I learned the hard way that although people were sincere about the advice they were offering me, they really had no idea what they were talking about.

You see, most people give advice based off their own personal experiences. They hear your story and dig deep into their own experiences and pain and tell you what (they think) you should do based off what they wish they had done or, in many cases, what they did. Sometimes, the person telling you what to do has never been in a situation that is even close to what you are going through. So, why do we listen to them? Why did I listen to them?

I was lost, plain and simple. I was also desperate. I wanted so badly to save my marriage that I would try anything I thought would help. For example, there was a couple with whom my then-husband and I had talked about our issues. This was before he left and we were still trying to work things out. They were a Christian couple, believers who had years of experience mentoring and guiding people. They traveled the country in a bus and preached about Christianity. Ernie and Louise had a long marriage of 40-plus years and seemed to be very knowledgeable. When they spoke to my husband and me, trying to help us in our marriage struggles, what they said made absolute sense and for about a week we were good again.

Unfortunately, my husband wasn't able to stay the course and went back to cheating and lying. When that same couple found out what was going on and I went to visit them to ask what I should do… well, I got what I asked for—ADVICE.

It turns out that this couple had a married daughter with a son. Through what sounded like a rough marriage to a bullying husband, their daughter was abandoned and left to raise her son on her own. While they were explaining this to me I could see the anger rising in Ernie and the sadness in Louise. They were still, understandably, very bitter about what had happened to their daughter. However, they were projecting that anger and bitterness into the advice they were giving me.

Of course, it was up to me whether or not to take their advice. They told me that I should take my kids and leave. And not just *leave*. They said I should go stay with their friends (that I did not know) in South Carolina. We lived in Arizona. It sounded crazy to me and I knew there was no way I could take my kids to South Carolina. So, I decided to go to my dad's house to stay a while. It was only a 90-minute drive, but it would get the point across. Ernie told me to give my husband what he wanted—his freedom—and show him what it was like to lose his family. I agreed, but driving away I felt more confused than ever.

I didn't want to leave my husband and I didn't want to drag my kids away from home. I wrestled with my decision all the way home. Driving home that afternoon I saw my husband's truck and horse trailer parked at a mountain trailhead just off the road. I knew he was riding to cool off after our argument that morning. Everything in me wanted to pull over and wait for him, to tell him how sorry I was. But, no… I had convinced myself that I had to do what Ernie and Louise told me to do. After all, they knew best. Didn't they?

The sad truth is that they did *not* know better and my gut instinct to stop and apologize and not leave home were correct. All my leaving did was give my husband justification to spend more time with his mistress. It gave him space and privacy to continue his affair. He did not once call to check on us or care at all that we were gone. The kids and I were miserable at my dad's house and we went home after two days. This was a major blow to our marriage and my husband did not come home. He continued to stay at his grandfather's house.

Therefore, it is so important to find a solid mentor/counselor. Someone who can be truly objective and who can guide you in making choices that are right for you. People will give you advice all the time and they sometimes won't even remember what they told you. Find someone who has your best interest in mind, and not someone who is reliving his or her past through you. Make sure you test what they are saying. If their advice is coming from the Bible, look up the scriptures and make sure what they are saying is true and correct. The Bible can lead you through any hard time you will ever encounter in life, and the advice and direction the Bible offers is solid and reliable. It has never failed me.

If you accept the gift of Jesus Christ that God offers all of us, then you will have a built-in guide, the Holy

Spirit. I believe it was the Holy Spirit urging me to stop and apologize that day and to not leave home. I regretted, with nausea and heartbreak, that I passed on the chance to stop and I will always regret not listening to what I *knew* was stronger and more aligned with what God would have me do than the advice of that couple. If I just ask myself, *What would God have me do?* and I read the Bible then I can solve many problems on my own and I can begin to keep myself on track. After a while this becomes habit and we can have a solid routine that keeps us on the straight and narrow and leading a positive life.

DON'T MAKE THE MISTAKES I MADE

Don't you love when you hear someone say, "I told them not to do that, but they had to learn for themselves the hard way." If you are like me, you have probably been on the hard-way end and had to learn for yourself. I have spent a lot of time there and have had to do a lot of repenting!

I have done so many things that I am embarrassed about. Some that other people know about; some I couldn't bear to say out loud so I keep those between God and me, even though I am positive He has forgotten by now. I would love to take every person who is separated or divorced and sit them down and say, "Please don't repeat the mistakes I've made, life will be hard enough without adding to the list."

Where do I begin? Let's ease into this with finances. I was a stay-at-home mother and two years prior to my divorce my husband, decided he was unhappy with his very well-paying job and wanted to quit and do something else. I wanted to support him and I hated to see him unhappy, so I agreed and we set out into a world of poverty we had not known since our early 20s. It sounds so much more romantic and exciting before reality sets in. My husband, after trying a few jobs, settled in as a rancher. It was something he grew up doing and loved. But, it didn't pay the bills very well and we had little left for enjoying life. At the time of our separation and divorce, we had no money saved and I had three small kids at home and only one of them was in school.

My husband supported me and the kids until our divorce was final, then we started the child support routine. I was so stressed about having to get a job and obsessed over the questions *What will I do with my children?* The town I lived in was a small one and I had little opportunity of getting a full-time job that would be able to cover child care expenses and still allow money to live. So, I got a credit card. *For emergencies only*, I told myself. Then, all of a sudden, everything felt like an emergency. By the time I married my second husband, I had an outstanding bill of $10,000 with the credit card company.

I had been so stressed out and was so ready to rely on only what I could humanly do, I forgot to look to God to see how He had planned to get us through this stage of our lives. Let me give you the play-by-play of how God always provided for us and how I messed it up... and how I am still paying for it.

My ex-husband offered to pay our house payment and give me $450 a month in child support. My car wasn't fancy, but it was paid for and ran well. And a piece of land we owned (that had been for sale for two years in a place where nothing was selling) sold around the time my divorce was final. I received nearly $5,000 as the down payment as well as $200 per month with a balloon payment due at the end of the second year.

It wasn't a lot of money, but it was enough if I had budgeted wisely. But for some reason, I couldn't do that. Blame it on my broken heart and lack of interest. One of my biggest issues was that I had always cooked dinner for my family and while I was cleaning the kitchen after dinner my husband wrestled with the kids on the floor. It was our everyday routine. And it was now no more. No more watching them be so silly while I put the dishes away and wiped down countertops. No more security in knowing my kids had a dad at their beck and call to play with. No more nightly routine and the comfort it gave me. So, I started taking the kids out to eat all the time. So much so that they started to hate going out to eat. I just couldn't bring myself to cook at night, it was too painful. Nonetheless, I should have sucked it up and cooked because my extra money soon dwindled and I was left with my small monthly income.

Even though I had money to pay my bills I would sometimes allow bills to go past their due date. Once my water was turned off, my health insurance was canceled, and so was my life insurance policy. For some reason I was not able to mentally discipline myself to be responsible with money, even though I had been a stickler for bill-paying and budgeting in the past.

This just goes to show that divorce will affect every aspect of your life. The best thing I could have done was seek out a responsible person to help me set a budget and have them hold me accountable. I strongly suggest this for you, my friend. If you have always been responsible with money and you feel as though you are fine and that nothing has changed, it still would not hurt to crunch numbers with a trusted resource.

I didn't only mess up in the numbers department; I also really messed up in the dating department. There I was, 32, divorced, and had never been with anyone except my now ex-husband. I had lost quite a bit of weight from running and being too sad to eat. In a weak moment,

I decided to bleach my hair blonde. I had time on my hands—which was something new that I wasn't used to—so I made sure every morning I did my hair and put on make-up. Something I hadn't done since before having my second child. In fact, I looked pretty, darn good... even though I felt dead inside. I went to the thrift stores to pass the time when I was alone and now had a new wardrobe and for the first time since before having kids I was a size 6 again. I looked good on the outside but felt awful inside.

The absence of a wedding ring and my new look gained the attention of more than a few men. I had never dated in my life. My first husband was my first real boyfriend. I had no idea what I was doing. I was still extremely naïve and felt that if someone told me something it was the truth. Boy, was I wrong. I was thrown into a dating world where people told you what they thought you wanted to hear. I believed them because I was telling the truth, so I assumed they were, too.

My first dating disaster came a few months after my divorce was final. I started going out with my best friend on nights when I didn't have my kids. We didn't drink but both of us had a love for music. So, we ended up at little bars around town that had live music. One night we were listening to a local singer I really liked, and who I thought was good looking. Through a few later encounters I ended up at his house one night. It had been almost a year since my husband left and with all the time I had on my hands I had romanticized how my first encounter with a new man might turn out. I was WRONG. It was awful. This guy was just that, a guy. I didn't know him well, I certainly didn't love him, and he had no interest in me other than sex. I though being with a new person would have some of the same feelings and emotions that being with my husband did.

This proved to me that a committed relationship, and most definitely a marriage, is the only place for sex. It took me two more mistakes just like that and a lying, cheating boyfriend to solidify that in my brain. I wish I had never ventured into that area. I wish I had waited until marriage, but I didn't. So, I have this opportunity to warn you not to make the same mistakes that I did in the romance department. There are many good people in the world who don't lie or cheat. Guys that aren't just after sex. You owe it to yourself to be picky and you must stay away from temptation. Because I liked to go out with my friend and listen to live music I put myself in a place where, honestly, men were just looking to hook up. And, when you have been rejected by your husband and abandoned, a nice-looking man who is obviously interested in you is a hard thing to resist.

With hindsight as a guide, this is what I would propose: Go out and have fun. If you enjoy music, listen to it. If you like hanging out at the lake, go for it. If you want to go on a cruise or lay on a beach for a week, do all those things. But what you should do first is realize how important *you* are. That's right, you are a treasure. And if you don't believe that look in the Bible at all the things God says you are. You are the King's daughter or son. You deserve to enjoy life. But you should be responsible. Talk with a friend you trust. Tell them about your plan for celibacy. Do you want to wait to have sex until you are remarried or at least in a very committed relationship? Tell this friend your weakness and temptations you need to stay away from. Have a plan of action for that friend to reel you back in if you feel yourself giving in. Get this laid out ahead of time with someone who will hold you accountable for your actions. It's not a babysitter, but sometimes we all need help to keep us on the straight and narrow. That's part of what a good friend can do.

The final trouble I would like to help you avoid involves texts, phone calls and social media. If you are like me, you struggle with wanting to make your ex feel like the terrible person that you know they can be. I really struggled with this and still do to a certain degree.

So, when you feel the urge to pick up the phone to start an argument or send a very long text about all the bad things they have done, don't. Plain and simple: don't. It's way easier said than done. I can attest to that. I started many a fight because I let my emotions run my mouth and my texting fingers. It seems safer to fight via text messages, since you can get every word in that you want to say, not get cut off, and not have to deal with their response. It is, in some ways, the perfect weapon. But the thing is, it is a weapon. That little tiny tongue in your mouth is a weapon also. It says in the Bible, James 3:8, "But no human being can tame the tongue. It is a restless evil, full of deadly poison." God warns us of our mouth as well. I can't tell you the times I wish I had not said anything because what ensued after I opened my mouth was nothing short of ugly. And, honestly, I never even got my point across. Somehow, if there ever really is a point to a phone message or a text, it gets lost in the madness and nothing is remembered except for the pain.

Please remember that even if your ex-husband was the most horrible person you could ever have imagined, you will be doing yourself and (if you have children) your children a disservice by continuing the war of words. You might use this standard to gauge your conversations by and what you should say: Is it true? Is it necessary? Is it building them up? For instance, instead of texting my ex-husband *you are a lying, cheating piece of crap who doesn't deserve our children*—and if I felt I really needed to say something—then I should say *I don't think this is the life God has planned for you and I worry about the affect it will have on our children.* But the truth is I don't care about actually saying that, the reason I (and probably you) want to contact an ex is because we are really hurting and we want them to know that they are the cause of that pain. We want them to care... and the fact that they don't care at all makes it even worse. So, save yourself some heartache and ease off on the unnecessary contact and work on healing your heart. Not everything we feel needs to be spoke in retaliation.

Finally, there is additional heartbreak that comes with social media. Sometimes I think it would have been so much easier to divorce in the '80s before all that amazing technology was available. Not only does it make our lives easier, it makes destroying our lives easier. How many times have you read a person's rant on social media about their ex or soon-to-be-ex and you think *Someone needs to let it go a little...* We've all been there, even if we haven't been the ones posting 'too much information' ourselves.

Social media is great to keep up with old friends, see pictures of loved ones, and find out about local events. But, social media can also be a tool that pushes us over the edge.

Case in point, I was on Facebook when a *Do you know this person?* picture popped up. It was her—my ex best friend and my ex-husband's new girlfriend, and it was a picture that I had taken of her. How could she use a photo I took of her! All I could think was ...*of all the low things to do.* That's when it got bad. I clicked on her profile. It was public, I could see everything. Not only was her relationship status listed as 'complicated,' clearly because she had been screwing her best friend's husband. That was my first thought, of course. The horror didn't stop there. She had posted what seemed like every picture she had ever taken of my kids on her page. Talk about one pissed off mother! I could barely reign in my emotions...

I immediately took to my Facebook page and blasted her. Not the highlight of my posting days and I am very embarrassed about doing so even though the comments I received were very supportive. The fact is, I set myself up by clicking on her page. Oh sure, I felt that tug in my gut telling me *this is a bad idea*, but I did it anyway. And you know what the result of all this madness was, I'm sure. I felt even worse about my life and I completely ruined one day of my life. No one did this to me, I did it to myself.

After being with someone for so long and having access to every part of them, it is hard to be cut off. And it's only natural to wonder what they are doing and who they are doing it with. It's really based in our insecurities. Are they having more fun without me? Is there new significant other better looking than me? How can they afford that trip when I can barely afford to take the kids to McDonald's? This is a sad, hard reality but it's true: Their life is no longer your business. It hurts me to say this so bluntly, but we need to let them go and live our own lives without them. So, I'd give serious thought to blocking your ex and their other on social media. Not forever, but until you are strong enough to read and see pictures without freaking out. You may have to include mutual friends or their family, just for a while. Consider it protection for yourself. In my case, it has been years since that happened and I still have them blocked, 'out of sight out of mind' is a good thing for me because it keeps me from doing something I would regret later.

IF YOU HAVE LEARNED A LESSON, YOUR TIME HAS BEEN WELL SPENT

Do you feel cheated, robbed of time? Does your heart sink when you think about all the time you invested in a relationship that did not work out? I feel this way sometimes. In the beginning, I felt it almost constantly. I would tell people that I invested 15 years of my life and now I have nothing to show for it. It wasn't until I said this to my friend Merrianne that she finished this statement correctly for me. She said, you invested 15 years of your life and you have three beautiful children to show for it.

She was right. Although, early on in the divorce process, the thought of having to share my kids with their father infuriated me. I felt as though he did not deserve to see them, that he made his choice, and the he shouldn't just get to drop by whenever he felt like it or be a part-time parent. And certainly not while I slaved away everyday trying to make our now-broken family work. But, she was right, I had three beautiful children to show for it and I would have to let that be enough.

How did I do it? I am positive I have not totally mastered this and, to some degree, I feel I never will. I had to learn how to accept the idea that it was ok for me to have put my heart and soul, blood, sweat and tears into a 15-year relationship that failed. Failure was probably the biggest obstacle in my way. I hated failing, it felt like quitting and I hated the idea of being a quitter. That is why I fought so hard to try and save my marriage. I can say without a shadow of a doubt that I did not quit or give up when it came to my marriage.

I realized this and thought, *Ok, this helps me deal with the idea of the 15 years I felt had been wasted.* It wasn't like I said one day, "You know I'm not very happy so I'm going to go ahead and tap out and see what else there is out there." I never gave up, I simply had to do what the court system and my ex-husband forced me to do. I was forced to move on, I was forced to let my marriage go. I can look my three little ones in the eye and tell them that I tried all that was humanly possible and that, in the end, it wasn't my choice.

In the end, it was someone else's choice and that makes it hard to deal with and accept. I am not one to have someone else make my choices for me, and it was hard to sit back and just react and respond. That was the only thing I could do, respond to paperwork regarding a long-time relationship. What a way to go. It wasn't even my choice and all I was able to do was respond to a packet of paper. I had trusted and loved this person and they betrayed and hurt me and ruined our family.

I would be enraged at the idea of those wasted years and often pondered why it all had to work out the way it did. After my pity parties were finished I would take a hard look at myself and the hours I spent reading and turning to the Bible for understanding and truth. Those truths and understanding God's plan for me would lead me to realize that my years were not wasted.

Reading the Bible, attending church and Bible studies, and having a Christian mentor started to help change my thinking. I started asking myself about the part I played in my breakup. From the outside looking in, it would appear that it was all my ex-husband's fault and that was easy to accept while I was hurting so badly. I started to separate my actions from his and could look at my faults with less emotion and more constructive criticism. After all, I wanted to be a better person. I wanted to be a good mom, a good friend, and a person who a potential husband could love and respect for a lifetime.

So, there I was thinking back on arguments, certain walls that had always been up in our marriage, my own attitude and how it affected situations. I did not like what I saw. I had been stubborn, driven to win at any cost, and so sure I was right that I would not even hear another side or point of view. There was no compromise with me, and I had a knack for cutting people down with the truth. And because it *was* the truth I felt justified in behaving that way. I also put my kids first and left little in my gas tank for my husband. I told myself when the kids get older we can get back to a better balance.

I saw an ugly version of myelf. I completely tore myself down for my past attitudes and behaviors and allowed my ex-husband to do the same. Then, I realized I had let the pendulum swing too far, now I was taking all the blame and allowing him to justify what he did with my words. The balance finally came when I allowed myself to forgive me. I confessed all my sins to the Lord and asked for forgiveness. He has been so kind in taking that burden from me and so wise to allow me the memory but not the pain. I have the memory so that I will not allow myself to repeat the past. But it did not happen quickly, it took many years. When a bad memory of something

I did to offend not only my ex-husband but anyone else would come to mind, I would confess it to the Lord, ask forgiveness, and file it in the Don't Do This Again folder I have stored in my brain.

I learned a lot over the past years and am thankful that I have so many years ahead of me to put what I have learned into practice. I am by no means able to say that I don't feel like I lost some time out of my life, but I am able to be still and focus on what I gained from those years. I do have three beautiful children and I see them developing into amazing young adults. I have found the kind of person I really want to be, the person I might never have discovered if I had stayed married.

It is my choice every day, I can choose to be bitter over time lost or choose to live in the present. After our spouses are no longer our husband or wife and we are left to face ourselves, then choosing to be bitter would only allow us to lose more time in our precious lives and we will only have ourselves to blame. My heartfelt message: Choose to live every day that you have left in this life in the best possible way you can.

ADD A LITTLE SUGAR TO THOSE LEMONS

You have undoubtedly heard it before: "When life gives you lemons, make lemonade." It is a simple statement, but it challenges us to find the sugar in our lives that will make those sour lemons into something sweet and refreshing. What is sweet and refreshing in your life?

When I was eight months into my separation and almost officially divorced I was miserable. I was still hoping my soon-to-be ex-husband would end the affair he was having and realize all that he was giving up—a family that dearly loved him and missed him terribly. I would pray that he would come home and that we could work on our marriage and go back to being the happy family I thought we were. The days were long and hard to get through and the nights were all too quiet and agonizing. I had a lot to be thankful for and I could name several things if I had to, but that took a lot of energy that I did not have. I had a lot of lemons in my life at the time, and it seemed no sugar was to be found to make that refreshing lemonade I so desperately craved.

One cold February day I had put my children—then four, five, and seven years old—down for a nap. I was thankful that I was still able to get all three kids to sleep at the same time because it gave me an hour or so of time when I didn't have to do anything. I could just sit. Sit and relax. When these short breaks occurred, I would try to get a little nap myself. But, like the last several months I was not able to sleep, day or night. I started crying and I hurt so bad on the inside it seemed I would never break free of this pain I felt. I loved and wanted a man who loved and wanted only what made him feel good. I was now raising three children on my own and I didn't even have the desire to get out of bed in the morning, let alone be a good mom.

As I laid there on that couch, crying, on that cold day I just couldn't make sense out of anything. My main thought was that I was all alone. I had never felt that kind of loneliness. The tears were pouring down my cheeks when, out of the corner of my eye, I spotted her, my innocent, little blonde-haired and blue-eyed baby girl. She stood there quietly, and I knew she could see I was upset. And I don't think she knew if it was ok for her to approach me. I wiped my eyes and turned to her. We didn't say anything to each other but with one look she came running over to me and jumped into my arms. She laid her head on my chest and I could feel the love she had for me pouring out of her tiny heart.

There we laid, tummy to tummy, just like when she was an infant and molded to my body when I held her on my shoulder. It was a flood of sugar to my soul, and in that instance, God showed me that I was not alone. And even though I had stockpiled lemons all over my life I had the perfect amount of sugar to go with them. I had three beautiful kids who loved me more than anything in their lives. They were the reasons I fought so hard to try to work out my marriage and not get divorced. They were the reasons I never gave up and the reasons I did get out of bed every morning. My house was a wreck, laundry was piling up, the yard was a disaster, and my emotions were a mess—but none of that mattered because I had been given three reasons to push through and get better… three reasons to survive.

I now knew that I had to focus on these little rays of sunshine that God had planted in my life. I had all the ingredients to make those sour lemons into some sweet, refreshing lemonade, all I had to do was focus more on the sugar God gave me than the sour, bitter things.

We started going on adventures, we lived close to the woods, so we went for walks. We enjoyed going to the movies, eating out at McDonald's so the kids could play with their friends and I could visit with mine. We had every-other-Friday-night pizza dates with my friend and her three grandchildren. As the days got warmer, we had outside BBQs. Life was slowly getting better as I focused on the good stuff.

I remember one day we went to the river and went on our first real hike. It was the first time I didn't have to carry a baby, all three could now walk on their own. I remember that day so well. Spring was beginning to make its entrance and the remnants of a cold winter were disappearing a little more every day. The afternoon sun was dipping behind the mountain and we could see the rays of sun peeking through and bouncing off the rocks and water. The sound of the rushing river made us feel alive and excited. We wanted to see what was around every corner, to explore every bend. I remember looking at those rays of sunshine that seemed to pierce through everything they touched, seeing the trees trying to form their buds as if waking up from a long winter's nap and hearing the birds chirping. It was a new beginning for every creature that day, including the four of us. I was now divorced, and we were learning to be on our own and accept our circumstances.

So, my question to you is what is the sugar in your life that you can focus on? For me it was obviously my kids, but there were other things too. Do you have children? If so, how is your relationship with them right now? Divorce is one of the hardest things a family can go through. It is the death of the only family a child has ever known. They are the innocent ones in the process. They don't know how to deal with what is going on and often one or both parents are belittling or speaking negatively about the other parent. If you have kids, then I challenge you to make them the sugar in your life. You will most definitely focus on something, so instead of focusing on the hurt, try and shift a little attention every day to be a more active, better parent. It doesn't happen overnight. I kept reminding myself that my kids were hurting too and by reading books on child rearing, attending classes on parenting, and trying to find out more about each child's personality and how to better individualize attention to that child, it will better help you to move on and bring about positive moments in your life.

What if you don't have children? Then what? I had this problem, too. For the first time in six years I had to learn to live without kids every other weekend and on some school breaks. And, for the first time in my adult life, I had to learn to be single. I had been with my husband since the summer before my senior year in high school. I had never lived alone. The first few seasons after my husband left and when the kids started visiting him every other weekend, I was a mess. I had terrible separation anxiety from being away from my children. I would take five hot baths a day every day my kids were gone and lie awake all night long. I counted the minutes until they would come home so my life would be 'normal' again.

Eventually I started trying to do things to keep myself busy when my children were gone. I had a horse that I helped to rehabilitate from an injury and I started riding him. It was scary, since I had never gone out on a horse alone, but at the same time it was amazing. Here we were, this thousand-pound animal and me, tromping through the woods enjoying all the beauty there was to see and both feeling like we were recovering—me from my divorce and him from his injury. I also made sure I kept the horse corral cleaned, which forced me to be active and outside in the sunshine. When I was sad or lonely it always helped to go outside for a walk or a run, to clean the yard, or just sit on the steps and enjoy the fresh air. It always made me feel better, feel like there was hope.

I also had Wednesday night dates with my best friend. We would go see a movie and enjoy a dinner together. It felt good to be in the company of only an adult sometimes. We talked and laughed, we cried and complained but we always walked away feeling better. We built a bond when we spent all those Wednesday nights together and we always looked forward to relaxing and having a fun evening out.

Soon after my husband had left our home I began spending more time with my family… my mother, father, and especially my brothers. Since I had been married at the age of 19 I had always lived in a different town than most of my family, especially in the last seven years of my marriage. I realized that because of my husband's attitude towards traveling with kids and taking the time to go out of town to visit my family and his fear of being in crowded places I had severely neglected quality time with my family. My niece and nephews had grown up not knowing me very well and I really missed the close relationship I once had with both my brothers.

On the weekends my kids were not home with me I started visiting my brothers more and when the kids were home we also made time to spend with my family. It was great. I went out dancing with my brother and taught him how to country dance. I met my brothers at the lake and we went out on the boat and enjoyed the hot Arizona weather. Reconnecting with the two boys who I will always consider my best friends was both an exciting adventure and a very powerful healing process. We are still very close, and I am thankful that in losing a man who did not care about me all that much, I found two men who had always loved and adored me more than anything.

Time passed, and I was adjusting to being officially divorced. My best friend and I were spending the free time I had without children together and having a great time. Don't get me wrong, it was still a very difficult time for me. But when we made plans and did exciting new things neither of us had ever done before it gave us both something to look forward to and helped me to stay positive about my new life.

Our first big adventure was Las Vegas. Oh boy, was that an experience—and not the thrilling one I thought it would be. We took my brother along and my friend ended up feeling a little sad and stayed in the room most of the time contemplating her life. My brother and I stayed out all night the first night just walking around and taking in the sights. It was fun. We paid for it the next day because our energy was sapped, and we went to sleep at about 8:00 pm. So much for the big party. The next morning before we left we went to ride the rollercoaster at New York, New York. We had a long wait to check out and get our car, so my brother and I went over to the rollercoaster while my friend got everything ready for us to leave.

Well, we both looked at the rollercoaster and started to chicken out. We just kind of looked at each other… and shrugged. As we started to walk away I stopped and told him, "No one will ever expect you and me to ride this rollercoaster, so that's what we are going to do." My moment of bravery took us all the way to the point of being strapped into the seats. Apparently, once you are strapped in and the rollercoaster starts moving is the wrong time to change your mind. There was no going back now. It was not a long ride, and we loved every minute of it! It felt amazing, the fear of the heights we were at and the stealing of my breath as we raced straight down. It was something I was terrified to do and something I needed to prove to myself I wasn't scared to try new things. We have a photo that captured that heady experience and we had our mouths wide open screaming and terrified looks on our faces—but we had the time of our lives and I wouldn't trade that memory for anything. I look at that picture often and smile.

CELEBRATE YOUR VICTORIES, NO MATTER HOW SMALL

It is so easy to be hard on ourselves. Oftentimes—and probably too often—we measure ourselves by our failures. What could we do better, how can we please the people in our lives more, why didn't I do this instead of that? These and many more questions bombard our thoughts every day. We have a case of the coulda, shoulda, woulda!

How about we start looking at things from a different point of view. Throw out the standards that everyone else sets for us. Standards or expectations like *you should be over this*, or you *shouldn't still be crying all the time... why can't you get your stuff together yet?* If you aren't hearing these comments from others, then chances are you are repeatedly telling yourself those things over and over in your head.

Instead of being so hard on yourself and concentrating on what you can't do, celebrate what you *are* doing right now. I remember before my husband left I was a good house cleaner and loved to work in the yard. Yes, we had a six-, a four- and a three-year-old so the house was usually strewn with toys. But, the laundry was always done, the kitchen and bathrooms were clean, and, overall, I kept up on all the chores quite well. After my husband left I didn't have the motivation to do anything. I did what I had to do and the rest fell by the wayside. I was embarrassed about how dirty my house was becoming, but just wasn't able to pull myself out of the funk I was in to do anything about it.

Then, I had an eye-opening moment. I always used my own bathroom and didn't go into the kid's bathroom much. When I did one day I realized I hadn't cleaned it at all in about three weeks and it showed. And, if you have or have had a little boy, you know how dirty a bathroom can get. I was so ashamed, I felt so bad that my children had been using such a filthy bathroom. Of course, I beat myself up about it. But I also got in there and scrubbed that room from top to bottom and I never let it get that way again. Every time I cleaned it I felt a sense of accomplishment. It seems silly that I would be so excited over cleaning the bathroom but every time I did it reminded me that I was winning the battle against my sadness and isolation.

I also let the yard go. I was the one who had always done all the yard work. I loved being outside and taking an unkept, unruly landscape and transforming it into something beautiful. Once my husband left, though, I had no interest and no energy to take care of our little acre. Instead, I started tending to the horse corrals that we had on our property. I had always pitched in and cleaned the corrals, but now it was my sole responsibility. It started as a chore and grew to be an enjoyable time for me. I would get out my rake, shovel, and wheelbarrow and start at one end and work my way to the other. Before long, I could look back and see progress. Seeing progress is something I celebrate. It was a little victory for me every time I could get out there and clean. My kids would usually come out with me and play while I cleaned so we all enjoyed the fresh air and sunshine and felt better afterward.

We had a large hill on the bottom half of our property and I would strategically dump the horse manure in certain places with future landscaping ideas in mind. As I would wheel my loads back and forth I would dream up different ways to landscape the property one day. Even though I didn't have the energy or motivation at the time to even think about landscaping, it felt good to keep the corrals clean and have my dreams about 'someday.'

These little victories made me feel proud and I should have celebrated them more than I did, because soon enough a little voice would pop up say, *the house still isn't clean enough, there are loads of laundry to be done, the yard is a mess* and so on. Then, there are the ongoing thoughts of *stop crying all the time*. A way to combat the added pressure of this idea is to think about your day and look for times when you didn't cry. For instance, I cried all the time, I just couldn't help it, in private or in public. I would be at church or the grocery store and start bawling. But, I finally saw progress when I stopped crying at church and, then, at most other public places. This was a big deal for me. Is it a big deal for you? Take a moment in the evening and think about the progress you are making. It may be so small that no one else notices, but that doesn't matter. All that matters, is that you notice, and you can be proud of yourself for continuing to get healthy.

Whether it is crying, being late for work, not wanting to do anything with your friends, whatever the case may be... it will get better. Don't think you are pathetic because you were late to work twice this week, celebrate that it was *only* two times and keep striving to be on time every day. If you haven't felt like doing anything make a date with a friend and tell them to drop by and pick you up, that way it is harder to get out of it at the last minute or duck out early. Even if it's only once a month, congratulate yourself on taking those little steps.

We tend to get stuck in the 'somedays' of our life. *Someday* I will feel better and start doing things I enjoy again, *someday* I will follow up on an activity I wanted to try, *someday* I will be more motivated and I will do it then. Remember that life is not only about the arrival, but how we get there. Do you want to be 90 and say at least I survived this life or do you want to be able to look back and say, some days were hard but I never gave up and I enjoyed the moments I could? Divorce is hard, it takes its toll on our heart, soul, energy, motivation and quality of life. Start today and embrace the positive things you see in your life. We can all do better in life, divorced or not, but that doesn't mean we should put ourselves down. I just kept trying and refused to give up.

I NEED SOMETHING TANGIBLE

Whether you are a Christian or not I am sure you have heard the phrase *hold onto God or just rely on Jesus... God is all you need right now* or something along those lines. Depending on the state of your heart and how much you are hurting this can be insulting or comforting, a statement that can infuriate you or bring calm and peace. If you are like me it can have different affects at different times.

In the beginning it was easy to hold onto Jesus, a piece of cake to rely on God. But, as time pushed on and things were not going the way I thought they would go (or the way I thought God would want them to go) it became harder to rely on God. I never stopped believing, though. In fact, my belief and love for God became stronger. But those words took on a whole new meaning. I had been relying on God to pull me through, but I only wanted the end result that I desired, when it did not work out the way I had hoped I still hung onto Jesus, but those statements gnawed at my insides.

Late one cold winter's night I sat on my bed after a shower and burst into tears. I was so lonely I could not stand it. I had put all my trust in God, but I was still so lonely. Then it dawned on me, I needed God to be tangible. I needed to see Him, sit next to Him, talk to Him and when I was feeling better after our visit, give Him a big hug. Well, as you know this was not possible for me. I won't be in God's presence until my time on earth is up. So, you can see my dilemma: I needed something I could see and feel with my own human eyes.

A couple weeks ago I was meeting with my mentor and she was telling me about a mutual friend who was also divorced. That friend had just broken up with her boyfriend and was alone again. Our mentor told her to trust in God. Our friend said that is easy to say when you have a husband to go home to at the end of the day. Bingo! It is very easy to tell someone to just trust in God when everything in your life is going well. It is sometimes very hard to rely solely on God when you have spent another sleepless night alone and hurting.

It is a fact that even though Adam, the first human created by God, could see and touch and talk to God in the Garden of Eden, he still became lonely. Can you believe this guy? He gets to walk and talk to God in the most beautiful garden in creation. He is given dominion over all the animals on earth and he is still lonely. So, what does our Maker say about this? In Genesis 2:18, God says "It is not good for the man to be alone. I will make a helper who is just right for him." We must understand that God understands our loneliness and he sympathizes. That does not mean that He will bring you a brand-new mate and things will be instantly better. But, if you continue to trust in Him and a new spouse is the desire of your heart, then I am fully certain that He will bring that to you when He feels you are ready.

I don't think we realize that God *is* tangible, in a way. We can look around and see the beautiful creations he has made, the sunsets, the ocean waves crashing on the shore, the endless stars in the sky. We can also touch Him, when we wrap our arms around a sweet, innocent child and feel a truly pure love. We can talk with Him through people He places in our lives, like best friends, counselors, mentors, and family. We can feel His arms around us when we are sad, when our parent lets us fall into their arms. You see, God created everything good, and if we can remember to see God in all the good in our lives then He can become tangible to us.

I know what it is like to feel so alone and long for an intimate, close love. As you recover from a divorce and focus on bettering yourself you will long for more fellowship with the Lord and have more peace rather than focus on finding a new spouse. I did go on dates and have relationships but none of them felt right and I made a lot of really big mistakes along the way. I have to say that my desire to be with someone did go away and ceased to be the main focus in my life. I wish I would have relied on God more and less on needing something tangible in my life to fill my voids, because if I had taken the time to really look I would have seen that God had been tangible to me all along.

LIFE ISN'T ALWAYS UNFAIR

"Guess what, Stace, life's unfair" That's what my husband said to me when I told him ...*that's not fair.* He had stopped by our house to tell me that he only wanted to see the kids every other weekend and Wednesday afternoons to help me out with work. I had a lowly $50-a-week, Wednesday-afternoon paper delivery route. I was a stay-at-home mom and had been for the last seven years. In my early 20s, I had a good-paying job with benefits and a few side jobs. My husband worked for the Forest Service and he wanted to move up the ladder, so that meant we would have to move. Either to a small town about an hour and a half's drive away or all the way to Utah. We chose the closer of the two and stayed in Arizona. He told me that if we focused on his career and made the move it would put us in a position to be able to start a family. A big family is all I ever wanted, so I was in. We both felt it was important for me to stay home and raise the kids. We didn't want our children growing up in day care, so we were very cautious with our plans.

But, then, there he was—standing in front of me— and all his priorities had changed. His new-found desires and freedoms had put our kids on the back burner. He told me I was going to have to get a job too. I asked, "What do I do with the kids?" and told him "This is not fair." That's when he told me, "Life's not fair." That is the moment I lost any respect I had left for him, which wasn't much at that point. Not caring about me was one thing; not caring how the kids would be taken care of made me sick to my stomach.

For the next three years that statement resonated in me. I took that saying to heart, and through all my trials and mistakes would always say to myself *Life isn't fair*. The one day I was searching the internet listening to music. I came across a song by Jarrod Niemann called *I Hope You Get What You Deserve*. This song totally flipped my thought process about the 'life's not fair' upside down. It is about a man talking to his ex…

For whatever reason, this song triggered the merciful side of me that day and I realized that life can be fair sometimes, that the pain we endure and the trauma we live through can be brought full circle and used for good.

Like the Bible says in Romans 8:28, "And we know that God causes everything to work together for the good of those who love God and are called according to his purpose for them." (NLT)

What we perceive as unfair at the time can be used by God for a greater and better purpose. I hated having to get a job, not because I am a lazy person. But because of having to leave my children. I was their mother and I did not want anyone else raising them. They were recovering from the loss of a full-time father and the thought of them having to lose out on time with me as well made me feel like the worst parent on earth.

I'll tell you this though, I worked six different part-time jobs with odd hours so that I would not have to leave my children in day care or at a babysitter's house. There were times when I did have to leave them for long hours at my parents' house, but I tried to limit that as much as possible. I was exhausted from the odd hours that I worked, but I can look back now and appreciate that I was with my children as much as possible.

It was unfair to have to work all those hours and raise the three kids by myself, but it was a good lesson for me. I realized that, in the past, I had taken for granted the opportunity to stay home and raise my children. I had, at times, complained about all the house work I had to do and how hard it was to raise babies while my husband was at work all day long. Don't get me wrong, it is absolutely hard work to keep a clean house and raise babies. It is more than a full-time job and it comes with little appreciation or kudos. But, after being left no option but to work, I realized how thankful I was to have had the opportunity to be home for seven years with my kids.

After I was remarried, I continued to work for a year and a half and then came to my husband one day and explained how important it was for me to spend more time at home with the kids. Remember, these were not his biological children. And I am so blessed that he absolutely agreed. I was able to cut my hours to only eight a week. I truly understand now how God does use everything for good. If I hadn't had those years where I was forced to work, I would never truly appreciate how amazing it is to raise my kids and be available to them full time.

Life can appear to be unfair, but if you trust in the Lord and stay on the narrow path, He will bring you peace in all those unfair situations. He won't always right those situations like you would hope, but over time you will see how your solution would not have been the best and that the way things are working out, although difficult, can grow you into a healthier, stronger person. Not only that,

He will use all those experiences to enrich your life and teach you invaluable lessons.

So, the next time you are stuck in a truly unfair situation, if you take the high road and do what God would want you to do, eventually that situation can be used for good in your life. I know it can feel like the whole world is coming down on you during or after a divorce, but all the things that happen—good and bad—are part of your story and what you choose to do with them can build you into a rock-solid person or shatter you into a million pieces. I have chosen to let unfair situations do both. Let me tell you, it is much harder to recover when we let others tear us down and dwell on it than it does to pick ourselves up and look for what could make us a stronger, wiser, and better person.

Life can seem unfair and not all situations seem to right themselves. Those are the ones we need to turn over to God because some things are just beyond our understanding... or there is really nothing that is needed from that situation to make us better. The art of trusting God to give us what we need when we need it can allow us to let go of a hurtful, unfair situation and move on.

Interestingly (and perhaps surprisingly) I found that through writing letters I was finally able to let go of some of the unfair pain that I was harboring. Maybe you have heard this before and thought it sounds so silly. I thought so too, but I have come to realize that it does work. I remember one time I was so angry at my husband's mistress. After all, she had been my best friend, she knew my children, we had shared close details of our lives together, and had fun doing things together. How could she betray me like this—and then have the nerve to tell me she had nothing to do with my divorce and that it was my fault because I was a bad wife. It seemed unfair to me. One day when I couldn't take it anymore I grabbed a pen and paper and started writing. At first, the writing was legible but by the fourth handwritten page my handwriting was so sloppy and the pages were tear-soaked almost to the point of not being able to decipher what was written. When I was done I curled up in a ball on the floor and had a good cry. I took that letter and all the pain associated with what I had written and I sat in front of the fire and burned it. Yep, I never mailed it to her. She doesn't have any idea I ever wrote it and it would seem that it was a pointless task. But it was extremely freeing. I said everything I wanted to say, and I felt as though the pain had left me and was transferred to those pages. I felt as though it would have been destructive to send a letter as true and honest and mean as the one I had written, so

I said a prayer and asked God to take this pain away and then burned it. For the most part, the pain is gone. There are times when I can think about it and get a little angry and hurt, but God has shown me who these two people who were so important in my life at one time really are and I am thankful not to be around them. Writing that letter really helped me let go of the unfair situation I had been in, so if you are struggling with letting some things go then give it a try. I would just caution you to prayerfully consider whether it is worth sending or is something that should be kept between you and God.

CHAPTER 16

OWNING YOUR PART AND GROWING HEALTHIER

I think the worst part of going through a divorce or recovering from a divorce is that a person feels like they will never shake the pain and misery that they feel. I think we feel like we will just somehow learn to live with it and go on. I am here to tell you that those feelings are merely a season, and not here to stay. You can always look back on something and feel sorrow or failure or sadness. But the agony will pass and then you go back to living your life.

It is healthy to be able to recall empathy and sympathy for a situation you have gone through in the past. I think having that ability makes us remember where we have been and how far we have come. It can also guide our actions, positively or negatively, the choice of how we handle challenges and heartache in our lives will always be ours.

Do I want to verbally rip my ex-husband to shreds when I recall the past and how he hurt me so badly? Yes, I do. Do I want to hurt my ex-friend as badly as she hurt me when I think of how she betrayed me? Yes, I do. But those feelings are just that, feelings. After I start to make myself feel ill by thinking how badly I would love to hurt those two, the truth sneaks in. I can always rely on the truth. And the truth is that they did me a favor. I would never want to have relationships with people who make conscious choices to deceive and cause pain— and who don't take responsibility for their actions.

The fact is, I am accepting of all kinds of people. People who have cheated, divorced, stolen, used drugs, and even physically and verbally abused another person. If I give it more thought, I'm sure I could add to this list. I know, it seems like such a double standard. How could I be friends with those people and not accept my ex's behavior? It's simple, my ex-husband and my ex-best-friend have shown no remorse, no repentance and have never even offered so much as an apology to me or my children. The others I know who have done similar things have clearly shown remorse and taken responsibility for their actions. They admit their faults and show a willingness to change, a desire and commitment to be better. Kind of like myself.

I could lump myself into the same category of cheater, liar, manipulator and so on. I would like to think that when I found my husband was cheating was when God gave me a huge wake up call. You see, I absolutely take responsibility for my actions that contributed to the breakdown of my marriage. It didn't just happen overnight. Years of stubbornness on my part and an unwillingness to see my own faults contributed to a wall in my marriage. I take full responsibility for that and when God started showing me all the situations that I could (and should) have handled differently, I would call or go see my ex-husband and explain what I did and apologize.

Can you imagine that? My husband was having a full-blown affair with a girl I thought was my best friend and I would make continuous calls to apologize to him. It seems superhuman, and it was. Only with the help of Jesus Christ, who forgave me for all my sins and continues to forgive me, could I find the strength to apologize and not expect anything in return. You see, I usually got no reaction from my ex when I apologized, not so much as a word from his lips. God showed me how to do the right thing at the expense of my pride and humility. I must say, it is one of the most humbling experiences we will ever encounter... finding the courage to ask someone who has hurt us badly for forgiveness. But God shows

His unwavering mercy and will extend a feeling of peace that you could never imagine.

I am not saying that a person should be a doormat or take the blame for everything, though I have done that as well. I encourage you to truly and without emotion look at your actions and evaluate what you could have done differently. And ask forgiveness from the offended party. You don't have to drag it out and ask repeatedly. If you can ask forgiveness from both Jesus and the party, you have offended—and repent—then you should give yourself permission to stop feeling guilty. Guilt does not come from God. Guilt is something that Satan would love for you to torture yourself with for the rest of your life. I urge you to be careful… because there is a fine line between forgiveness from the Lord and feeling you are off the hook and can do whatever you want. This is when we usually repeat the same mistake over again. We don't have to feel guilty, but we should feel a sense of responsibility to take care in not repeating our mistakes.

I have had the experience of seeing so many people ask forgiveness from the Lord only to go out and repeat the same actions again and again. I myself have had times when I would do the same thing. It is like a merry-go-round. We sin, then ask forgiveness, then sin, then ask forgiveness. It is a cycle that we should all be aware of and careful to avoid. If you find that you are constantly asking forgiveness for the same sin, you may want to seek help, you don't need to do this on your own. It is so important to have a Christian mentor in your life. A person who is not necessarily your best friend, but someone who knows God's word, someone you can trust, and with whom you can be very honest. This person should be someone who will hold you accountable and help you through your problems with firm Christian love and support. If you really want to break the cycle of sin, then you need to have Godly guidance.

Once you stop the cycle of sin and start apologizing and letting God shape you into the person He wants you to be, then the pain and agony of divorce is going to slowly be replaced with peace that only God can give you. While you are going through the process you are going to hit some major roadblocks. It's your choice as to how you will handle them. You can drive like a madwoman and bust through them, only to be turned around later to repeat the same drive. Or you can sit patiently and let God show you what you need to work through to get past these obstacles and challenges. Sometimes, if you choose to wait it will feel like you are stuck on the freeway in Phoenix, Arizona on a hot June day with no air conditioning... uncomfortable to say the least. Other times you will decide you have had enough and choose to blast through that roadblock, only to have a police officer stop you, give you an expensive ticket, and send you to the back of the line to wait it out. On paper, it seems much easier to wait it out, but in real life and real time I think you will find it to be a very hard choice!

The process of finding the things in us that need tending to, nurturing, and changing is slow. God will not give us more than we can handle, so if you are presented with a situation that you think is way too much to take in, remember that the Lord knows you are ready to deal with it. The situation may bring up old pain you thought you had tucked tightly away, never to be seen or heard from again. But that pain needs to be faced for us to continue to grow into better versions of ourselves. The old saying 'slow and steady wins the race' is true in this case. With the proper support system of mentors, counselors, a church family, and healthy friends you will overcome the hurdles you face and grow into a stronger, healthier person.

CHAPTER 17

TAKE CARE OF YOURSELF

It was a hard road to travel, this whole divorce process. It left me weakened and not caring what happened to me. Most days it was a struggle to take care of my children, and I rarely thought about my own health. I am here to tell you that you need to absolutely take care of yourself—your health—during this process.

I have never really felt well, my whole life. I can remember when my symptoms started. I was in fifth grade and I was tired all the time. I used to pretend I was sick so I could stay home. Looking back now I realize that was my first encounter with depression as well. This cycle has continued my whole life. The feeling of complete exhaustion accompanied with bouts of depression, weight gain, and always being cold down to the bone in winter. Also, I would constantly feel like I was getting the flu, but it would go away if I could get some extra rest.

Finally, in 2006, I was diagnosed with Hashimoto's disease, an autoimmune disease that attacks the thyroid. I was finally being medicated properly and was feeling better, but not well. I was also diagnosed with postpartum depression after having my third child in 2006. The combination of an antidepressant and thyroid medication enhanced the quality of my life.

When the suspicion of an affair and the fighting that followed began I could feel my body changing. I felt like I had an adrenaline rush that a person would get when they are scared. I had this feeling constantly. I was nauseous all the time which made me lose complete interest in food. I had digestive problems, my menstrual cycle was irregular, and even though I was exhausted all the time I could not sleep. I felt anxious and realized later that anxiety attacks were a part of everyday life for me now.

I felt that now my husband no longer cared about my health or what happened to me and would use the fact that I was taking an antidepressant against me. So, I went off my medication. Just at the time in my life when I probably needed it the most. But, I didn't want to give my husband any reason to try to take my kids away from me. I decided I would suffer through it.

I did not eat well, and I wasn't able to sleep. This combination went on for a few years. I could feel my body grow weaker and I was down to a weight I hadn't been at since junior high school. Although I looked good on the outside, my body was shutting down. I grew more and more fatigued. This would go on for years. I would tell my doctor that I felt exhausted and she would tell me that my blood test looked good, that nothing was wrong with my thyroid levels. So, I just figured this was my life and it all must be in my head, so I pushed through.

Finally, in 2015, after living with these problems for almost six years I sought a naturopathic doctor and we had an hour discussion about what was going on with me. Through a complete blood test, she found that I was in adrenal failure, I had no iron in my body, no D3 in my body and low testosterone. This was such a breakthrough for me. It wasn't in my head, there was something truly wrong with me. It took a year and, with all-natural supplements and a lot of extra sleep, I brought my body back into the normal range and felt like my quality of life increase dramatically.

This was all because I didn't take care of myself. I didn't eat right, get enough sleep, and I didn't seek out a different doctor soon enough. I suffered for six years needlessly. Although my body reacting to stress from my divorce, was not something I could completely control. And there were steps I could have taken to ensure my body would have what it needed to stay healthy.

I'm certain that what you are feeling before, during, and after your divorce is most likely normal. I can't stress to you enough that this rollercoaster of emotions will take its toll on your body in a very unhealthy way. I urge you to go see your doctor and let him or her know how you are feeling. You may not need medication, and there are many great all-natural products that can support your body during this overwhelming time. You shouldn't be exhausted and feeling ill all the time. Please, my new friend, take care of yourself so you can begin to live a beautiful life again.

WHERE PAIN ENDS AND PEACE BEGINS... A NEW LIFE FOR YOU

My divorce was final In February 2010. It is now nearly a decade later, and I'm looking ahead to the start of a new year. I have waited a very long time to finish this book. I'm not sure why. I have been very busy with life, but I don't think that is the reason. I feel called by God to share my story, so it can bring help and healing to others, but I seem to have taken a long time to do that. I can only accept the fact that I completed this book when the time was right... when I was ready to share my story and my journey. Sometimes, it is easy to hide away, hide our pain and emotions. When we do that we don't get better or grow.

In a way, I feel as though sharing this information makes me vulnerable in a way that seems overwhelming. Sometimes I think, what if my neighbor, friend, pastor or (heaven forbid) kids get a hold of this book. Then they will know these personal details of my life. On the other hand, I think, I could have followed what God was prompting me to do this whole time then I could have helped people who were hurting. That saddens me.

Where am I now? I have been married for five years. I have a fourth child, who is now four. My little ones I spoke of aren't so little anymore. They are now 16, 14, and 13. I completely agree with the statement "The days are long, but the years are short." I remember having to get through moment by moment and breath by breath when my separation with my first husband started. Now, the only time I think of that time is when my three older kids are hurting. I moved on and love my husband and four children and am able to not let the divorce take much of my time, but my kids still struggle with the loss of our family. I don't blame them. We have an entirely new set of problems, but we are able to function normally with the set of circumstances we have been given.

I still have the choice every day to be bitter or be better. I don't want to be bitter. Some days I will make a rude remark about the parenting style of my ex to my best friend or husband, but I don't want negativity to dominate my life so those are few and far between. I just want what is best for my children. So, I try to be civil and polite.

I can look back and see that It would have never worked out if my ex-husband and I would have tried to reconcile. I see that God was taking me to a place my ex was not ready to go. I pray, for my kid's sake, that in time my ex-husband finds the life God would love for him to have, but the days of worrying about him are over and I know that worrying is no longer my responsibility.

I have settled into the new life God has for me and I found a man with whom I was able to build a solid friendship first and someone who, like me, bases decisions on what God would have us do. Neither of us is perfect and we both know this. I think that is why we work so well together, we are completely flawed, and we have both accepted that. We don't just rely on one another for our happiness, instead we are a team and neither player is more important than the other. We strive to be better and look forward to what God has in store for us. We both come with our own set of problems, but we are willing to be patient and work on our relationship.

I remember back in December 2009, in the depth of my misery, when I stayed awake all night reading a book. When I finished I felt compelled to write down a thought I had. I grabbed a pen and wrote in the back of that book. The strange thing is it had nothing to do with the book I just read. I know what I wrote was straight form God and it still stands true today. It says: *We are given a formula to follow. If we believe and pray in God's perfect will then He can do anything and change anyone. We hold out for "God's best." I have come to the realization that my best is certainly not "God's best" ... and how can I expect "God's best" from someone who has free will, is human, and refuses to embrace Christ one hundred percent? I am judging them too harshly if I expect them to be Christ-like when I myself, embracing Christ to the best of my ability, will never be Christ-like. Every now and then people will see Christ working through me, but I will never obtain the ultimate goal here on earth. If we can truly say we have given our best, is it then ok by God to bow out of our situation and begin a new life. I don't believe anyone on earth can answer that. I do believe that it is ok because otherwise He would not have given us repentance, forgiveness, grace and mercy.*

We are human, we live in a fallen world. I have done my best and it is time to begin a new life. It is time to accept that it is ok for others to begin a new life as well. I believe in God's best. I have seen Him work miracles and I know He weaves everything together in ways that are best for us. Maybe "God's best" is to take the worst possible situation in your life and bring about peace and goodness, even if it means painfully moving on. We are never defeated if we hold Jesus in our heart.

In marriage we vow to forsake all others. This was not the case for me, I was forsaken. There were many days and months I felt alone and discarded. I wondered, *Was God listening to me?* I knew He loved me, but would he answer my prayers?

The beauty in hindsight is that looking back over those years, I can say with confidence is that God was truly with me every step of the way. He heard my prayers and I am in awe of the outcome and the way He helped me through this time.

Yes, I have been forsaken, you may feel this too. In writing this book—*Forsaken*—I am hoping to pass on to you the spirit and freedom of that beautiful spring day when my children and I started our new lives. I can still feel that crisp air on my face and the joy filling my soul. I can still look up and see the sun piercing all aspects of the day: the blue sky, the rays bouncing off the mountains, and the sparkle of the water. It is a reminder that God is always with us shining His guiding light.

ABOUT THE AUTHOR

STACEY PRICE

Stacey Price has been writing since she was 11 years old. She has amassed suitcases full of her writings and journal entries. She was inspired to write her first book after going through an extremely difficult divorce. Stacey felt that if she could to share her experiences, good and bad, she might help people who are also struggling with the difficult times in their lives. She found that she had a knack for sharing emotions and events that helped shape and define her life in hopes of inspiring others through their hard times in life.

Today Stacey has an amazing husband and four beautiful children, five dogs, two cats, two rabbits and a horse. Life is full and busy with two teenagers, a preteen and an almost-four-year-old. There are ups and downs in life, especially in a blended family, but there is always beauty in the storm.

Being a mother is her favorite and most important job and if she could leave her children with just one thought it would be that when you have the choice between being right and being kind, choose kindness.